단기간에 마무리하는 8가지 핵심 비법

woongjin compass

비법 담은 중학 영문법

3

특강편

비법 담은 중학 영문법 특강편 3

지은이 한길연, 이나영, 박영은
펴낸이 최회영
책임편집 김종원, 이승혜
감수 정은화, 김주희, 오승희, 이수진, 이지애, 정은숙
영문교열 David Charlton
디자인 디자인플러스
펴낸곳 (주)웅진컴퍼스
등록번호 제22-2943호
등록일자 2006년 6월 16일
주소 서울특별시 서초구 강남대로39길 15-10 한라비발디스튜디오193 3층
전화 (02)3471-0096
홈페이지 http://www.wjcompass.com
ISBN 979-11-6237-002-5

13 12 11 10 9 8 7 6 5 4
23 22

Photo Credits
All photos © Shutterstock, Inc.

Printed in Korea

CONTENTS

이 책의 구성과 특징

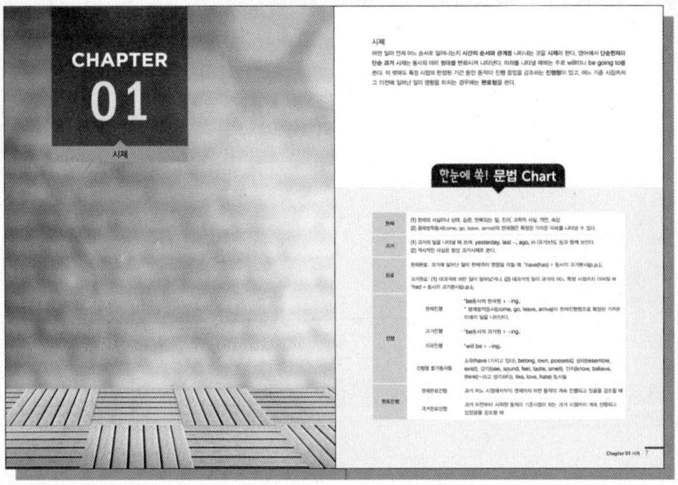

챕터 가이드

각 챕터의 학습 목표, 배울 내용과 함께 중요한 문법의 개념과 용어를 한눈에 보기 쉽도록 정리하였습니다.

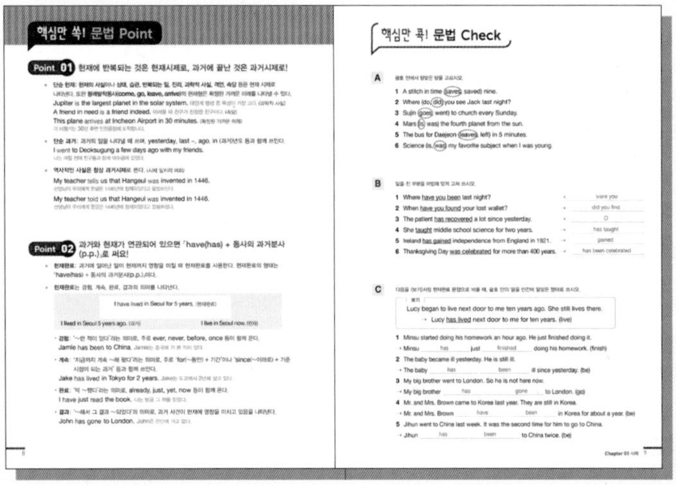

핵심만 쏙! 문법 Point

쉽고 정확한 문법 설명과 최신 교과서의 구문을 반영한 실용적인 예문을 제공합니다.

핵심만 콕! 문법 Check

앞서 배운 문법을 다양한 유형의 문제로 풀어보며 다시 한번 확인하도록 합니다.

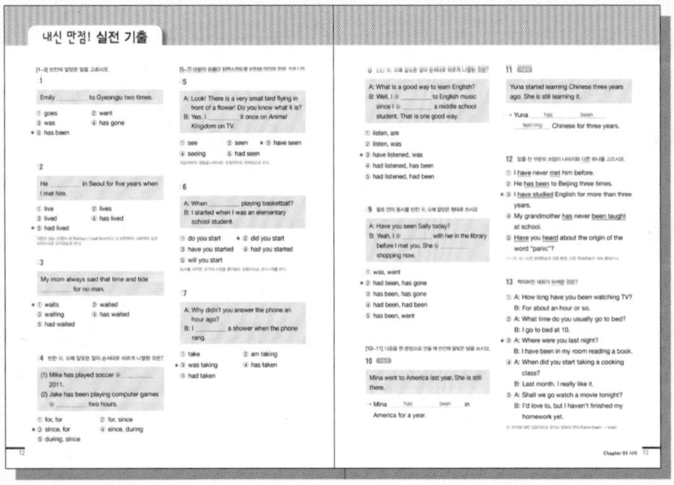

내신 만점! 실전 기출

최근 7년 전국 중학교 기출문제를 최다 빈출 문항 위주로 제공합니다. 또한 비중이 커진 수행평가를 위한 서술형 문제와 고난도 문항까지 완벽 대비합니다.

목차

CHAPTER 01

시제

시제

어떤 일이 언제 어느 순서로 일어나는지 **시간의 순서와 관계**를 나타내는 것을 **시제**라 한다. 영어에서 **단순 현재**와 **단순 과거** 시제는 동사의 어미 형태를 변화시켜 나타낸다. 미래를 나타낼 때에는 주로 will이나 be going to를 쓴다. 이 밖에도 특정 시점의 한정된 기간 동안 동작이 진행 중임을 강조하는 **진행형**이 있고, 어느 기준 시점까지 그 이전에 일어난 일이 영향을 미치는 경우에는 **완료형**을 쓴다.

한눈에 쏙! 문법 Chart

현재	(1) 현재의 사실이나 상태, 습관, 반복되는 일, 진리, 과학적 사실, 격언, 속담 (2) 왕래발착동사(come, go, leave, arrive)의 현재형은 확정된 가까운 미래를 나타낼 수 있다.	
과거	(1) 과거의 일을 나타낼 때 쓰며, yesterday, last ~, ago, in (과거)년도 등과 함께 쓰인다. (2) 역사적인 사실은 항상 과거시제로 쓴다.	
완료	현재완료: 과거에 일어난 일이 현재까지 영향을 미칠 때. 「have(has) + 동사의 과거분사(p.p.)」	
	과거완료: (1) 대과거에 어떤 일이 일어났거나, (2) 대과거의 일이 과거의 어느 특정 시점까지 이어질 때 「had + 동사의 과거분사(p.p.)」	
진행	현재진행	「be동사의 현재형 + ~ing」 * 왕래발착동사(come, go, leave, arrive)의 현재진행형으로 확정된 가까운 미래의 일을 나타낸다.
	과거진행	「be동사의 과거형 + ~ing」
	미래진행	「will be + ~ing」
	진행형 불가동사들	소유(have (가지고 있다), belong, own, possess), 상태(resemble, exist), 감각(see, sound, feel, taste, smell), 인지(know, believe, think(~라고 생각하다), like, love, hate) 동사들
완료진행	현재완료진행	과거 어느 시점에서부터 현재까지 어떤 동작이 계속 진행되고 있음을 강조할 때
	과거완료진행	과거 이전부터 시작된 동작이 기준시점이 되는 과거 시점까지 계속 진행되고 있었음을 강조할 때

핵심만 쏙! 문법 Point

Point 01 현재에 반복되는 것은 현재시제로, 과거에 끝난 것은 과거시제로!

- **단순 현재: 현재의 사실**이나 **상태, 습관, 반복되는 일, 진리, 과학적 사실, 격언, 속담** 등은 현재 시제로 나타낸다. 또한 **왕래발착동사(come, go, leave, arrive)**의 현재형은 확정된 가까운 미래를 나타낼 수 있다.
  Jupiter is the largest planet in the solar system. 태양계 행성 중 목성이 가장 크다. (과학적 사실)
  A friend in need is a friend indeed. 어려울 때 친구가 진정한 친구이다. (속담)
  This plane arrives at Incheon Airport in 30 minutes. (확정된 가까운 미래)
  이 비행기는 30분 후면 인천공항에 도착합니다.

- **단순 과거**: 과거의 일을 나타낼 때 쓰며, yesterday, last ~, ago, in (과거)년도 등과 함께 쓰인다.
  I went to Deoksugung a few days ago with my friends.
  나는 며칠 전에 친구들과 함께 덕수궁에 갔었다.

- **역사적인 사실은 항상 과거시제**로 쓴다. (시제 일치의 예외)
  My teacher tells us that Hangeul was invented in 1446.
  선생님께서 우리에게 한글은 1446년에 창제되었다고 말씀하신다.
  My teacher told us that Hangeul was invented in 1446.
  선생님께서 우리에게 한글은 1446년에 창제되었다고 말씀하셨다.

Point 02 과거와 현재가 연관되어 있으면 「have(has) + 동사의 과거분사(p.p.)」로 써요!

- **현재완료**: 과거에 일어난 일이 현재까지 영향을 미칠 때 현재완료를 사용한다. 현재완료의 형태는 「have(has) + 동사의 과거분사(p.p.)」이다.
- **현재완료**는 경험, 계속, 완료, 결과의 의미를 나타낸다.

I have lived in Seoul for 5 years. (현재완료)

I lived in Seoul 5 years ago. (과거) I live in Seoul now. (현재)

- **경험**: '~한 적이 있다'라는 의미로, 주로 ever, never, before, once 등이 함께 온다.
  Jamie has been to China. Jamie는 중국에 가 본 적이 있다.
- **계속**: '지금까지 계속 ~해 왔다'라는 의미로, 주로 'for(~동안) + 기간'이나 'since(~이래로) + 기준 시점이 되는 과거' 등과 함께 쓰인다.
  Jake has lived in Tokyo for 2 years. Jake는 도쿄에서 2년째 살고 있다.
- **완료**: '막 ~했다'라는 의미로, already, just, yet, now 등이 함께 온다.
  I have just read the book. 나는 방금 그 책을 읽었다.
- **결과**: '~해서 그 결과 ~되었다'의 의미로, 과거 사건이 현재에 영향을 미치고 있음을 나타낸다.
  John has gone to London. John은 런던에 가고 없다.

핵심만 콕! 문법 Check

A

괄호 안에서 알맞은 말을 고르시오.

1 A stitch in time (saves, saved) nine.
2 Where (do, did) you see Jack last night?
3 Sujin (goes, went) to church every Sunday.
4 Mars (is, was) the fourth planet from the sun.
5 The bus for Daejeon (leaves, left) in 5 minutes.
6 Science (is, was) my favorite subject when I was young.

B

밑줄 친 부분을 어법에 맞게 고쳐 쓰시오.

1 Where <u>have you been</u> last night? → ______________
2 When <u>have you found</u> your lost wallet? → ______________
3 The patient <u>has recovered</u> a lot since yesterday. → ______________
4 She <u>taught</u> middle school science for two years. → ______________
5 Ireland <u>has gained</u> independence from England in 1921. → ______________
6 Thanksgiving Day <u>was celebrated</u> for more than 400 years. → ______________

C

다음을 〈보기〉처럼 현재완료 문장으로 바꿀 때, 괄호 안의 말을 빈칸에 알맞은 형태로 쓰시오.

보기
Lucy began to live next door to me ten years ago. She still lives there.
→ Lucy <u>has lived</u> next door to me for ten years. (live)

1 Minsu started doing his homework an hour ago. He just finished doing it.
→ Minsu ____________ just ____________ doing his homework. (finish)
2 The baby became ill yesterday. He is still ill.
→ The baby ____________ ____________ ill since yesterday. (be)
3 My big brother went to London. So he is not here now.
→ My big brother ____________ ____________ to London. (go)
4 Mr. and Mrs. Brown came to Korea last year. They are still in Korea.
→ Mr. and Mrs. Brown ____________ ____________ in Korea for about a year. (be)
5 Jihun went to China last week. It was the second time for him to go to China.
→ Jihun ____________ ____________ to China twice. (be)

핵심만 쏙! 문법 Point

Point 03 과거 이전부터 시작되어 과거까지 영향을 주면 「had + p.p.」!

- **과거완료**: 과거완료는 두 과거 시점을 연관 지어 표현할 때 쓴다. 특정한 과거 시점보다 더 이전에 일어난 과거를 대과거라고 한다. 즉, 과거완료 형태는 (1) 대과거에 어떤 일이 일어났거나, (2) 대과거의 일이 과거의 어느 특정 시점까지 이어져서 경험, 계속, 완료, 결과를 나타낼 때 쓴다. 형태는 **「had + 동사의 과거분사 (p.p.)」**이다.

  I didn't go to the cafeteria because I had already eaten something.
  나는 이미 뭔가를 먹어서 식당에 가지 않았다.
  Before I started writing the report, I had finished the research.
  보고서 작성을 시작하기 전에 나는 조사를 마쳤다.

Point 04 어떤 일이 어느 시점에 진행 중이면 진행형으로!

- **진행형**은 기준 시점에 진행되고 있는 일을 나타낸다. **현재진행**은 **「be동사의 현재형 + ~ing」**으로, **과거진행**은 **「be동사의 과거형 + ~ing」**, **미래진행**은 **「will be + ~ing」**의 형태로 쓴다.
  I am looking for a bag online. 나는 온라인으로 가방을 찾아보고 있어. (현재진행)
  He was trying on a pair of jeans. 그는 청바지 한 벌을 입어보고 있었다. (과거진행)
  I will be studying when you come back. 네가 돌아올 때는 나는 공부를 하고 있을 거야. (미래진행)

- **왕래발착동사(come, go, leave, arrive)**의 **현재진행형**으로 확정된 가까운 미래의 일을 나타낸다. 이 때 tomorrow, next week 등의 가까운 미래를 나타내는 시간 표현과 대개 함께 쓰인다.
  They are leaving this country next month. 그들은 다음 달에 이 나라를 떠날 것이다.

- **소유, 상태, 감각, 인지 등을 나타내는 동사는 진행형으로 쓰지 않는다.**

진행형으로 쓰지 않는 동사	소유, 상태 동사	have (가지고 있다), belong, own, possess, resemble, exist
	감각, 인지 동사	see, hear, feel, taste, smell, know, believe, think(~라고 생각하다), like, love, hate 등

  Do you think modern technology has benefited humans?
  Are you thinking modern technology has benefited humans? (x)

  cf. 단, 상태, 감각 등을 나타내는 동사도 위와 다른 뜻으로 동작을 나타내거나 주어의 의지가 강한 일시적인 동작, 상태임을 강조할 때에는 진행형으로 쓸 수 있다.
  I am thinking of giving up my part-time job. (think: ~을 생각하다, 고려하다)
  People are having lunch on a boat. 사람들이 배 안에서 점심을 먹고 있다. (have: 먹다)

Point 05 과거의 일이 현재까지 진행중임을 강조하려면 「have been ~ing」로!

- **현재완료진행**은 과거 어느 시점에서부터 현재까지 어떤 동작이 계속 진행되고 있음을 강조할 때 쓴다. 형태는 **「have/has been + ~ing」**이다.
  Irish people have been celebrating St. Patrick's Day for more than 1000 years.

- **과거완료진행**은 과거 이전부터 시작된 동작이 기준시점이 되는 과거 시점까지 계속 진행되고 있었음을 강조할 때 쓴다. 형태는 **「had been + ~ing」**이다.
  I had been playing a computer game before my mom entered my room.

핵심만 콕! 문법 Check

A 괄호 안에서 알맞은 말을 고르시오.

1 When I arrived at the station, the subway (left, had left) a few minutes before.
2 What (are, were) you doing when he visited you?
3 I (feel, am feeling) that we are being treated unfairly.
4 He (is, will be) giving a speech when you arrive there.
5 They (have, are having) a simple device to clean water.
6 We (know, are knowing) that some scientists have invented things to help poor countries.
7 It's true that more than 6000 people (are, were) dying every day from drinking dirty water.

B 밑줄 친 부분이 어법에 맞으면 O표, 틀리면 바르게 고쳐 쓰시오.

1 They <u>were having</u> a nice big house then. → ____________
2 What <u>are you thinking</u> of Korean culture? → ____________
3 She <u>is wearing</u> a T-shirt and blue jeans now. → ____________
4 We <u>are having</u> dinner at this time tomorrow. → ____________
5 The train for Cheonan <u>is leaving</u> on track two in 5 minutes. → ____________

C 우리말과 뜻이 같도록 괄호 안의 말을 활용하여 문장을 완성하시오.

1 그는 엄마에게 받은 용돈을 다 썼다. (receive)
→ He spent all the allowance that he ________ ________ from his mom.

2 Mike는 한 시간째 수영을 하고 있다. (swim)
→ Mike ________ ________ ________ for an hour.

3 그녀가 오기 전에, 나는 이미 저녁을 먹고 있었다. (eat)
→ Before she came, I ________ ________ ________ dinner.

4 너는 지금까지 얼마나 오랫동안 TV를 보고 있었니? (watch)
→ How long ________ ________ ________ ________ TV so far?

5 Jessie는 9시부터 계속 사무실에서 일하고 있다. (work)
→ Jessie ________ ________ ________ in her office since 9 o'clock.

내신 만점! 실전 기출

[1~3] 빈칸에 알맞은 말을 고르시오.

01

Emily __________ to Gyeongju two times.

① goes ② went
③ was ④ has gone
⑤ has been

02

He __________ in Seoul for five years when I met him.

① live ② lives
③ lived ④ has lived
⑤ had lived

03

My mom always said that time and tide __________ for no man.

① waits ② waited
③ waiting ④ has waited
⑤ had waited

04 빈칸 ⓐ, ⓑ에 알맞은 말이 순서대로 바르게 나열된 것은?

(1) Mike has played soccer ⓐ __________ 2011.
(2) Jake has been playing computer games ⓑ __________ two hours.

① for, for ② for, since
③ since, for ④ since, during
⑤ during, since

[5~7] 대화의 흐름이 자연스럽도록 빈칸에 알맞은 말을 고르시오.

05

A: Look! There is a very small bird flying in front of a flower! Do you know what it is?
B: Yes. I __________ it once on *Animal Kingdom* on TV.

① see ② seen ③ have seen
④ seeing ⑤ had seen

06

A: When __________ playing basketball?
B: I started when I was an elementary school student.

① do you start ② did you start
③ have you started ④ had you started
⑤ will you start

07

A: Why didn't you answer the phone an hour ago?
B: I __________ a shower when the phone rang.

① take ② am taking
③ was taking ④ has taken
⑤ had taken

08 빈칸 ⓐ, ⓑ에 알맞은 말이 순서대로 바르게 나열된 것은?

A: What is a good way to learn English?
B: Well, I ⓐ __________ to English music since I ⓑ __________ a middle school student. That is one good way.

① listen, am
② listen, was
③ have listened, was
④ had listened, has been
⑤ had listened, had been

09 괄호 안의 동사를 빈칸 ⓐ, ⓑ에 알맞은 형태로 쓰시오

A: Have you seen Sally today?
B: Yeah. I ⓐ __________ with her in the library before I met you. She ⓑ __________ shopping now.

① was, went
② had been, has gone
③ has been, has gone
④ had been, had been
⑤ has been, went

[10~11] 다음을 한 문장으로 만들 때 빈칸에 알맞은 말을 쓰시오.

10 서술형

Mina went to America last year. She is still there.

→ Mina __________ __________ in America for a year.

11 서술형

Yuna started learning Chinese three years ago. She is still learning it.

→ Yuna __________ __________ __________ Chinese for three years.

12 밑줄 친 부분의 쓰임이 나머지와 다른 하나를 고르시오.

① I have never met him before.
② He has been to Beijing three times.
③ I have studied English for more than three years.
④ My grandmother has never been taught at school.
⑤ Have you heard about the origin of the word "panic"?

13 짝지어진 대화가 어색한 것은?

① A: How long have you been watching TV?
B: For about an hour or so.
② A: What time do you usually go to bed?
B: I go to bed at 10.
③ A: Where were you last night?
B: I have been in my room reading a book.
④ A: When did you start taking a cooking class?
B: Last month. I really like it.
⑤ A: Shall we go watch a movie tonight?
B: I'd love to, but I haven't finished my homework yet.

최다빈출

14 어법상 옳은 문장은?

① The phone rang, but she couldn't hear it.
② Susie is shocked when she heard the news.
③ Mr. Park has been teaching English in 2000.
④ I have lived in Busan before I moved to Seoul.
⑤ Jessie always got up at six and goes jogging.

15 어법상 어색한 것은?

① Have you been to Africa?
② He has never tried bungee jumping.
③ My team has won the game yesterday.
④ It's been a long time since we last met.
⑤ Did you know that Mark had won the writing contest?

16 밑줄 친 부분의 쓰임이 나머지와 다른 하나는?

① I am leaving for Daejeon tonight.
② Jina is coming home this weekend.
③ This plane is arriving in LA in 30 minutes.
④ We are preparing dinner in the kitchen now.
⑤ They are visiting Seoul National Museum tomorrow.

[17~18] 괄호 안의 말을 활용하여 우리말과 뜻이 같도록 문장을 완성하시오.

17 서술형

우리가 정거장에 도착했을 때 그 버스는 이미 떠났다. (leave)

→ When we reached the stop, the bus ___________ already ___________.

고난도

18 서술형

너는 '높이 나는 새가 더 멀리 본다.'라는 말을 들어본 적이 있니? (hear, see)

→ ___________ you ___________ the saying, 'A bird flying high ___________ further'?

19 어법상 틀린 문장을 모두 고르면?

ⓐ I have bought a nice jacket yesterday.
ⓑ She has gone to Paris several times on business.
ⓒ When you called me, I was watching a documentary.
ⓓ Mount Kilimanjaro was covered with snow all year round.
ⓔ Sumi has been practicing tennis for more than two hours.

① ⓐ, ⓒ, ⓔ ② ⓑ, ⓓ, ⓔ ③ ⓑ, ⓒ, ⓔ
④ ⓐ, ⓑ, ⓓ ⑤ ⓐ, ⓑ, ⓔ

[20~21] 어법상 어색한 부분을 찾아 바르게 고쳐 쓰시오.

20 서술형

엄마가 집에 돌아오실 때쯤이면, 나는 숙제를 마칠 것이다.
→ By the time my mom comes back home, I have finished doing my homework.

___________ → ___________

21 서술형

Jenny는 그녀의 엄마와 아주 많이 닮았다.
→ Jenny is really resembling her mother.

___________ → ___________

[22~23] 다음을 읽고 물음에 답하시오.

Jinsu: Are you okay?
Minji: (A) I have been sick for a week, and I still feel a little bit weak.
Jinsu: Oh, my! What was wrong?
Minji: I got wet in the rain last weekend, and (B) I had a bad cold since then.
Jinsu: (C) Have you been taking medicine?
Minji: Yes, I have. (D) A doctor prescribed some for me. It really helps.
Jinsu: You should go home early and rest.
Minji: (E) I have some research to do first, but I think that's a good idea.

신유형

22 위 글을 잘못 이해한 학생은?

① 수진: 민지가 지난 주말부터 지금까지 계속 아프구나.
② 민호: 민지는 아직도 좀 기운이 없어.
③ 찬수: 민지는 지난 주에 비에 젖어서 그때부터 심한 감기에 걸려 있구나.
④ 민영: 민지는 의사에게서 받은 처방약을 지금은 먹지 않고 있어.
⑤ 주호: 민지는 아직 조사할 게 좀 남았지만 일찍 집에 갈 거 같아.

고난도

23 위 글의 (A)~(E) 중 어법상 틀린 것은?

① (A) ② (B) ③ (C)
④ (D) ⑤ (E)

24 빈칸 ⓐ~ⓒ에 알맞은 말이 순서대로 바르게 나열된 것은?

A: Hi, Bill. How was your trip to Las Vegas?
B: It was great. My friends and I ⓐ (drove, has driven) through the desert to the Hoover Dam.
A: Wow! How long did that take?
B: It usually takes about 7 hours. But we visited several places on the way, so it took more than that.
A: Hmmm. How many times ⓑ (were you, have you been) there?
B: That was my first time. I ⓒ (has never been, had never been) there before.

① drove, were you, had never been
② has driven, were you, had never been
③ has driven, were you, has never been
④ drove, have you been, had never been
⑤ has driven, have you been, had never been

고난도

25 서술형 심화

Compare the two pictures. Complete the sentences using the given words. (You can change the word form if necessary. There are some extra words.)

보기
get have read since three hours for

→ Susie started reading a book at 3 o'clock. Now, it is 8 o'clock and it (1) __________ __________ dark. (2) She __________ __________ __________ a book (3) __________ __________ __________.

CHAPTER 02

to부정사

to부정사

「to + 동사원형」의 형태로 문장 안에서 명사, 형용사, 또는 부사의 역할을 한다. 주어의 인칭과 수에 따라 형태가 정(定)해지는 것이 아니고(不), 항상 「to + 동사원형」형태로 쓴다고 하여 to부정사(不定詞)라고 부른다.

- **to부정사의 다양한 용법 & to부정사의 의미상의 주어**

명사적 용법	My dream is **to be** a singer. (보어 역할)
	I don't know **where to go**. (목적어 역할)
형용사적 용법	I need **someone to help** me. (명사 수식)
부사적 용법	I am **glad to see** you again. (감정의 원인)
	He **grew up to be** an English teacher. (결과)
	She **must be rich to buy** such an expensive ring. (판단의 근거)
to부정사의 의미상의 주어	It is hard **for me** to get an A on the math test. (for + 목적격)
	It is nice **of you** to say so. (of + 목적격)

한눈에 쏙! 문법 Chart

용법	명사적	문장의 주어, 보어, 목적어역할	~하는 것/~하기	
		의문사 + to부정사	= 의문사 + 주어 + should+ 동사원형	
		가주어 it, 가목적어 it	문장의 주어 혹은 목적어로 쓰인 to부정사구를 대신하고, to부정사는 문장 뒤로 보낸다	
	형용사적	명사 + to부정사구	to부정사구가 앞의 명사 수식	
		명사 + to부정사 + 전치사	to부정사의 수식을 받는 명사가 전치사의 목적어인 경우 to부정사 뒤에 전치사 필요	
		~thing/one/body + 형용사 + to부정사	형용사가 뒤에 오는 명사를 to부정사가 수식할 때는 형용사 다음에 to부정사가 온다.	
		be + to부정사	예정, 의무, 가능, 의도, 운명의 뜻으로 쓰임	
	부사적	목적(= in order to, so as to), 감정의 원인, 판단의 근거, 결과, 형용사 수식, 조건		
의미상의 주어		to부정사의 행위의 주체가 문장의 주어나 목적어와 일치하지 않을 때	to부정사 앞에 for + 목적격	대부분의 경우
			to부정사 앞에 of + 목적격	사람의 성질이나 특성을 나타내는 형용사가 함께 쓰일 때
		to부정사의 행위의 주체가 문장의 주어나 목적어와 같거나, 일반인일 경우	의미상 주어 생략	
부정사의 부정		not(never) + to부정사		
시제		단순부정사 「to + 동사원형」	to부정사의 시제가 주절의 시제와 같을 때	
		완료부정사 「to + have + p.p.」	to부정사의 시제가 주절의 시제보다 앞설 때	
목적보어로 쓰인 to부정사		본동사가 대부분의 동사	to+동사원형	
		본동사가 사역, 지각동사	동사원형 (to가 빠짐)	
형/부 + enough to부정사 = so 형/부 + that + 주어 + can(could) + 동사원형			~할 만큼 충분히 ~하다, 충분히 ~해서 ~할 수 있다	
too + 형/부 + to부정사 = so 형/부 + that + 주어 + can't(couldn't) + 동사원형			너무 ~해서 ~할 수 없다, ~하기에는 너무 ~하다	

핵심만 쏙! 문법 Point

Point 01 to부정사는 문장에서 주어나 목적어, 또는 보어로 쓰여요!

- **주어 역할**: To have a true friend is important. 진정한 친구를 갖는 것은 중요하다.
  목적어 역할: She wants to buy a new bag. 그녀는 새 가방 사는 것을 원한다.
  보어 역할: My dream is to be a pilot. 내 꿈은 파일럿이 되는 것이다.

- 「의문사 + to부정사」는 「의문사 + 주어 + should + 동사원형」으로 바꿔 쓸 수 있다.
  I don't know how to make a snowman. → I don't know how I should make a snowman.

- 주어나 목적어로 쓰인 to부정사구가 너무 길면, 대개 **가주어 it** 또는 **가목적어 it**을 대신 쓰고 **진짜 주어/목적어인 to부정사구를 뒤로** 보낸다.
  To know yourself well(주어) is important. → It(가주어) is important to know yourself well(진주어).

  I found to speak Chinese fluently(목적어) difficult. → I found it(가목적어) difficult to speak Chinese fluently(진목적어).

Point 02 to부정사는 문장에서 형용사처럼 대명사를 꾸며주며, 주어를 보충설명 하기도 해요!

- **to부정사**는 앞에 나온 명사, 대명사를 꾸밀 수 있고, '~할,' '~하는'이라고 해석한다. (형용사 역할)
  It's time to go to school. 학교에 갈 시간이다.

- to부정사의 수식을 받는 **명사가 전치사의 목적어인 경우 「명사 + to부정사 + 전치사」**의 형태로 나타낸다.
  You write with a pen. → I bought a pen to write with. 나는 쓸 펜을 하나 샀다.

  You sit on a chair. → She needs a chair to sit on. 그녀는 앉을 의자가 필요하다.

- **형용사와 to부정사가 동시에 꾸며줄 때, 「-thing/-one/-body + 형용사 + to부정사」**의 순서로 쓴다.
  I want something (cold) to drink. 나는 마실 (차가운) 무언가를 원한다.

- 「**be동사 + to부정사**」형태로 '예정, 의무, 가능, 의도, 운명'의 다양한 의미로 주어를 보충 설명할 수 있다. 부정형은 「**be동사 + not + to부정사**」이다.
  (1) **예정**: ~할 예정이다 (= will, be going to)
  The movie is to start soon. 영화는 곧 시작할 것이다.
  (2) **의무**: ~해야 한다 (= must, have to)
  We are to follow the law. 우리는 법을 따라야 한다.
  (3) **가능**: ~할 수 있다 (= can, be able to)
  Nothing was to be seen in the park. 공원에서 아무것도 볼 수 없었다.
  (4) **의도**: ~할 작정이다 (= will, intend to)
  Study hard if you are to pass the exam. 시험에 통과할 작정이라면 열심히 공부해라.
  (5) **운명**: ~할 운명이다 (= be destined to)
  The soldier was to die in the World War II. 그 군인은 2차 세계대전에서 죽을 운명이었다.
  He was never to see her again. 그는 그녀를 다시는 만나지 못할 운명이었다.

핵심만 콕! 문법 Check

A 괄호 안에서 알맞은 말을 고르시오.

1 I can't decide (what, who) to eat.
2 (That, It) is difficult to make kimchi.
3 Please tell me (why, when) to call you.
4 It is dangerous (to drive, drive) too fast.
5 She has many friends (to play, to play with).
6 I have (something to give, to give something) you.

B 밑줄 친 to부정사의 쓰임 혹은 역할을 〈보기〉에서 찾아 쓰시오.

보기

ⓐ 예정　ⓑ 의무　ⓒ 가능　ⓓ 의도　ⓔ 운명

1 You are <u>to clean</u> your bedroom. → ______
2 Not a star was <u>to be seen</u> in the sky. → ______
3 The boxer was never <u>to be</u> a champion. → ______

보기

ⓐ 주어　ⓑ 목적어　ⓒ 보어

4 Mary's dream is <u>to become</u> a doctor. → ______
5 My best friend likes <u>to watch</u> movies. → ______
6 <u>To take</u> care of my baby sister is not easy. → ______

C 두 문장의 뜻이 같도록 「be동사 + to부정사」 구문을 활용하여 문장을 완성하시오.

1 I am going to ride my bike after school.
→ I ______ ______ ______ my bike after school.
2 They were destined to fall in love with each other.
→ They ______ ______ ______ in love with each other.
3 We must submit the final report by Friday.
→ We ______ ______ ______ the final report by Friday.

D 우리말과 뜻이 같도록 괄호 안의 말을 바르게 배열하여 문장을 완성하시오.

1 나의 취미는 만화책을 만드는 것이다. (to, comic, make, books)
→ My hobby is ______________________.
2 그녀의 계획은 세계를 배낭여행 하는 것이다. (to, backpacking, around the world, go)
→ Her plan is ______________________.
3 시험 공부를 할 시간이다. (is, to, time, study, it)
→ ______________________ for the exam.
4 회의는 이번 수요일에 열릴 예정이다. (held, is, be, to)
→ The meeting ______________________ this Wednesday.

핵심만 쏙! 문법 Point

Point 03 to부정사는 문장에서 부사처럼 쓰이기도 해요!

- 목적(~하기 위해서, ~하러): 「in order to + 동사원형」 또는 「so as to + 동사원형」으로 바꿔 쓸 수 있다.
  He saves money to buy a new car. 그는 새 차를 사기 위해 저축한다.
  → He saves money in order to buy a new car. → He saves money so as to buy a new car.
- 부정형(~하지 않기 위해): to부정사 앞에 not을 붙인다. 「in order not to + 동사원형」 또는 「so as not to + 동사원형」으로 바꿔 쓸 수 있다.
  She ran hard not to miss the train. 그녀는 기차를 놓치지 않기 위해 열심히 뛰었다.
  → She ran hard in order not to miss the train. → She ran hard so as not to miss the train.
- 감정의 원인(~해서, ~하니): I am glad to see you again. 나는 너를 다시 만나니 매우 기쁘다.
- 결과(~해서 결국 …하다/되다):
  My grandfather lived to be 100 years old. 나의 할아버지께서는 100세까지 사셨다.
- 판단의 근거(~하다니): 「must be + 형용사 + to부정사」의 형태로 쓰인다.
  Ben must be smart to act like that.

Point 04 to부정사의 의미상 주어는 「for + 목적격」 또는 「of + 목적격」을 써요!

- (1) to부정사 앞에 「**for + 목적격**」: 대부분의 to부정사에 사용한다.
  It is easy for her to understand the story. 그녀가 그 이야기를 이해하는 것은 쉽다.
  (2) to부정사 앞에 「**of + 목적격**」: to부정사 앞에 사람의 성격이나 주관적 평가를 나타내는 형용사 (nice, kind, smart, wise, silly, polite, rude, honest, thoughtful 등)가 있을 때 쓴다.
  It is nice of him to offer his seat to an elderly lady. 그의 자리를 노인에게 양보하다니 착하다.
- to부정사의 의미상 주어의 생략:
  I want to become a famous movie star. (문장의 주어 = to부정사의 의미상 주어)
  I want you to become a famous movie star. (문장의 목적어 = to부정사의 의미상 주어)
  It is bad (for people) to talk behind someone's back. (사람들이) 뒤에서 욕을 하는 것은 나쁘다.
- **to부정사의 부정**은 to부정사 앞에 **not** 또는 **never**를 붙인다.
  I decided not to talk about his faults any further. 나는 더 이상 그의 잘못에 대해 말하지 않기로 결심했다.
- **대부정사**: 동일한 동사구가 앞에 이미 나왔을 때, 뒤에 오는 to부정사의 동사를 생략하고 to만 쓸 수 있다.
  You can go home if you want to (go home).

Point 05 to부정사의 시제는 주절의 시제와 비교를 해서 정해요!

- 「**seem + to부정사**」: ~인 것 같다 = 「**It seems that + 주어 + 동사 ~.**」
  The tall boy seems to like you. → It seems that the tall boy likes you.
- **to부정사의 시제**
  (1) **단순부정사 「to + 동사원형」**: to부정사의 시제가 주절의 시제와 같을 때 쓴다.
  It seems **that** the old man is rich. → The old man seems to be rich. 그 노인은 부자인 것 같다.
  It seemed **that** the old man was rich. → The old man seemed to be rich.
  그 노인은 부자인 것 같았다.
  (2) **완료부정사 「to + have + p.p.」**: to부정사의 시제가 주절의 시제보다 앞설 때 쓴다.
  It seems that that boy argued with his sister.
  → The boy seems to have argued with his sister.

핵심만 콕! 문법 Check

A 괄호 안에서 알맞은 말을 고르시오.

1 Ann bought a ticket (to see, not to see) a movie.
2 I opened the window (of, for) fresh air to come in.
3 I got up early (not to be, to be not) late for school.
4 It is kind (of, for) her to help the senior citizen get a seat.
5 David went to China (so to learn as, so as to learn) Chinese.

B 밑줄 친 부분을 어법에 맞게 바르게 고쳐 쓰시오.

1 He ran fast <u>to not miss the train</u>. → ______________
2 He <u>decided to attend not the meeting</u>. → ______________
3 It is <u>impossible of me</u> to get up early. → ______________

C 각 문장의 뜻이 같도록 빈칸에 알맞은 말을 쓰시오.

1 She studied hard not to fail the exam.
→ She studied hard in ________ ________ ________ ________ the exam.
→ She studied hard so ________ ________ ________ ________ the exam.

2 It seems that the woman is an actress.
→ The woman ________ ________ ________ an actress.

3 Michael seemed to have been a painter.
→ ________ ________ ________ Michael ________ ________ a painter.

D 〈보기〉와 같이 to부정사를 활용하여 다음을 한 문장으로 만드시오.

보기
I was disappointed. I got a C in math. → I was disappointed to get a C in math.

1 The boy must be honest. He told the truth.
→ The boy must be honest ______________________________.

2 My aunt went to South Africa. She helped the poor children there.
→ My aunt went to South Africa ______________________________.

E 우리말과 뜻이 같도록 괄호 안의 말을 바르게 배열하여 문장을 완성하시오.

1 Tom은 금메달을 타서 매우 기뻤다. (win, very, to, happy)
→ Tom was ______________________________ a gold medal.

2 깊은 바다에서 수영을 하는 것은 위험하다. (in, swim, to, the deep sea)
→ It is dangerous ______________________________.

3 Terry는 시험에 떨어지지 않기 위해 열심히 공부한다. (not, fail, to)
→ Terry studies hard ______________________________ the exam.

4 그는 집들이에서 재미있었던 것 같다. (seems, have, to, fun, had)
→ He ______________________________ at the house warming party.

핵심만 쏙! 문법 Point

Point 06 to부정사는 문장에서 목적어와 목적격 보어로도 쓰여요!

- 「**동사 + to부정사(목적어)**」: 다음의 동사들은 **목적어로 to부정사를 취한다.**

동사 want, wish, hope, expect, plan, agree, mean, choose, decide, would like, learn, promise 등	+	to부정사

I hope to enter Seoul National University. 나는 서울대학교에 입학하기를 희망한다.

- 「**동사 + 목적어 + to부정사**」: 다음의 동사는 **목적격보어로 to부정사를 취한다.**

동사 want, ask, tell, allow, expect, order, advise, encourage 등	+	목적어	+	to부정사

(~에게 …하도록 원하다/부탁하다/말하다/허락하다/기대하다/명령하다/조언하다/용기를 북돋우다)

My mom **always** tells me to make my bed. 엄마는 항상 내게 침대를 정리하라고 말씀하신다.

Point 07 지각, 사역동사의 목적보어로는 동사원형이 와요!

사역동사 make, have, let 등	+	목적어	+	동사원형

(~에게 …을 시키다/~하게 하다/허락하다)

The red light made people stop crossing the street. 빨간 불은 사람들이 길 건너는 것을 멈추게 했다.
She had her son finish his homework. 그녀는 그녀의 아들이 숙제를 마치도록 했다.
Let me check the password. 내가 비밀번호를 확인할게.

- **help**는 목적격 보어로 to부정사와 동사원형 둘 다 올 수 있다.
  He helped me (to) find the building. 그는 내가 그 건물을 찾도록 도와주었다.
- **get**은 사역동사의 의미를 갖지만 목적격 보어로 to부정사가 온다.
  He got her to clean the house. 그는 그녀에게 집을 청소하게 했다.

지각동사 see, look at, watch, hear, listen to, smell, feel, notice 등	+	목적어	+	동사원형 / 현재분사

(~가 …하는 것을 보다/듣다/냄새 맡다/느끼다/알아차리다)

I saw the baby cry/crying. 나는 아기가 우는 것을 보았다.

Point 08 「too~ to」와 「enough to」는 자주 쓰이는 to부정사 구문이에요!

- 「**too + 형용사/부사 + to부정사**」는 '너무 ~해서 ~할 수 없는, ~하기에는 너무 ~한'이라는 뜻이며 「**so + 형용사/부사 that + 주어 + can't(couldn't)**」로 바꿔 쓸 수 있다.
  The male athlete is too slow to break the record.
  → The male athlete is so slow that he can't break the record.
- 「**형용사/부사 + enough + to부정사**」는 '~할 정도로 충분히 ~한'이라는 뜻이며, 「**so + 형용사/부사 that + 주어 + can(could)**」으로 바꿔 쓸 수 있다.
  He is strong enough to carry the books. → He is so strong that he can carry the books.

핵심만 콕! 문법 Check

A 괄호 안에서 알맞은 말을 고르시오.

1 I saw him (dance, danced) in the rain.
2 My teacher advised me (to study, studied) harder.
3 The class president made the students (be, to be) quiet.
4 They want (to buy, buying) new furniture for the living room.
5 My brother helped me (finishing, to finish) the science homework.

B 밑줄 친 부분을 어법에 맞게 고쳐 쓰시오.

1 She wishes <u>studying</u> abroad. → ____________
2 Let me <u>helping</u> you. → ____________
3 I could smell something <u>burned</u>. → ____________
4 The hot chocolate is <u>too to drink hot</u>. → ____________
5 She heard the kitten <u>to cry</u> at night. → ____________
6 Tom helped me <u>moving</u> the furniture. → ____________

C 두 문장의 뜻이 같도록 문장을 완성하시오.

1 He is strong enough to move the desk.
→ He is so ______ ______ ______ ______ move the desk.

2 Jenny was smart enough to pass the test.
→ Jenny was so ______ ______ ______ ______ pass the test.

3 The new student is too shy to make friends easily.
→ The new student is so ______ ______ ______ ______ make friends easily.

4 The backpack is too small to hold all my textbooks.
→ The backpack is so ______ ______ ______ ______ hold all my textbooks.

D 괄호 안의 말을 바르게 배열하여 문장을 완성하시오.

1 그는 그의 아들이 컴퓨터 게임을 하도록 허락했다. (his, allowed, son, play, to)
→ He ____________________ computer games.

2 그는 웨이터에게 물 한잔을 가지고 오도록 시켰다. (had, bring, the waiter)
→ He ____________________ a glass of water.

3 날씨가 캠핑을 가기에는 너무 춥다. (go, too, to, cold)
→ The weather is ____________________ camping.

4 Ben은 경주에서 이기기에 충분히 빠르다. (enough, fast, to, win)
→ Ben is ____________________ the race.

5 나는 누군가 나를 노려보는 것을 느꼈다. (at, someone, stare, felt)
→ I ____________________ me.

내신 만점! 실전 기출

01 빈칸에 알맞지 않은 것은?

She __________ him study English after school.

① let ② saw ③ had
④ told ⑤ made

02 빈칸에 알맞은 것을 모두 고르면? (2개)

I saw him __________ a gold medal in the English Speech Contest.

① win ② wins ③ to win
④ win to ⑤ winning

03 서술형

우리말과 뜻이 같도록 괄호 안의 말을 활용하여 빈칸에 알맞은 말을 쓰시오.

그녀는 버스에 탄 첫 탑승자가 되어 기뻤다. (become)

→ She was happy ______________ the first passenger to get on the bus.

04 빈칸에 알맞은 말은?

One piece of paper is not enough for me __________ all my wishes on.

① write ② writing ③ to write
④ writing on ⑤ to write with

05 서술형

두 문장의 뜻이 같도록 빈칸에 알맞은 말을 써서 문장을 완성하시오.

I wish to learn how I should play the flute.

→ I wish to learn ________ ________ ________ ________ ________.

06 빈칸에 알맞은 말이 순서대로 바르게 나열된 것은?

- She wants ⓐ __________ to Paris during the winter vacation.
- Tony's mom allowed him ⓑ __________ computer games.

① travel, to play ② to travel, play
③ to travel, to play ④ traveling, to play
⑤ to travel, playing

07 서술형

다음 문장을 주어진 말로 시작하여 다시 쓰시오.

It seems that Mrs. Wilson hates her children's bad habits.

→ Mrs. Wilson seems ______________________________.

08 어법상 틀린 문장은?

① I found it dangerous drive fast.
② It is important to have a dream.
③ It is not easy to fix the computer.
④ It is hard to answer the question.
⑤ It is impossible for me to finish it by noon.

09 서술형

우리말과 뜻이 같도록 괄호 안의 말을 활용하여 문장을 완성하시오. (필요하면 형태를 바꿔 쓸 수 있음)

그 챔피언은 스스로를 자랑스러워하는 듯 보인다. (be proud of oneself)

→ (1) The champion seems to ______________________________.

→ (2) The champion seems that ______________________________.

10 두 문장의 뜻이 같도록 빈칸에 알맞은 말은?

It seems that he is one of my neighbors.
→ He __________ one of my neighbors.

① seemed to
② seems that
③ seems to be
④ seems being
⑤ seems to have been

11 to부정사의 쓰임이 ⓐ와 같은 것은?

In the 1960s, many Korean nurses and miners went to Germany ⓐ to work.

① She always wants to play badminton.
② Give me a racket to play badminton with.
③ She says that she plays badminton to have fun.
④ It is not so easy to win the badminton match.
⑤ There were many things to buy in the supermarket.

12 서술형

「so ~ that …」 구문을 활용하여 밑줄 친 ⓐ를 완전한 영어 문장으로 다시 쓰시오.

A: What's wrong with Sally?
B: ⓐ Her parents are too poor to pay her school tuition.

→ ______________________________
____

최다빈출

13 어법상 옳은 문장은?

① It is generous of him to say so.
② It was silly for me to fail the exam.
③ It's nice for her to help other people.
④ It's hard of me to get up early in the morning.
⑤ It is dangerous of them to go out late at night.

14 서술형

「의문사 + to부정사」 구문을 활용하여 ⓐ를 영작하시오.

Tomorrow is my mom's birthday. So I want to buy a birthday gift for her with my older sister. ⓐ 나는 언니를 언제 만날 지 모른다.

→ I don't know ______________________________
______________________________.

15 어법상 틀린 문장을 모두 고르면? (2개)

① He wants to be famous.
② I decided to study harder.
③ She agreed starting after lunch.
④ I'd like you think about your future.
⑤ They expect to see the speaker again one day.

16 서술형

우리말과 일치하도록 괄호 안의 말을 활용하여 영작하시오.
(단, 필요한 단어를 하나 추가하시오.)

그녀는 그에게 함께 먹자고 부탁했다.
(him, eat, together, she, asked)

→ ______________________________
____

17 문장의 의미가 나머지 넷과 다른 하나는?

① It was too cold to swim in the river.
② I was very cold, so I could swim in the river.
③ It was so cold that I couldn't swim in the river.
④ It was very cold, so I couldn't swim in the river.
⑤ Because it was too cold, I couldn't swim in the river.

최다빈출 고난도

18 빈칸 어디에도 들어갈 수 없는 하나는?

> (1) She called me to ask ________ spaghetti.
> (2) I'm done. Please tell me ________ the school.
> (3) I'm sorry to hear your bad news. I don't know ________ to you.
> (4) Can you give me a hand? I really don't know ________ this problem.

① what to say
② how to solve
③ how to make
④ when to leave
⑤ where to meet

[19~20] 밑줄 친 ⓐ와 쓰임이 같은 것을 고르시오.

19

> The best way to know yourself is ⓐ to find out what you are good at. It may help you understand yourself better and find a suitable job.

① I need something to drink.
② His hobby is to take photographs.
③ She studied hard to pass the exam.
④ He went to France to see the Eiffel Tower.
⑤ You should know yourself to find the right job.

20

> My family went camping except my sister. She had to prepare a group project, so she didn't have time ⓐ to join us. I hope she will go with us next time.

① They want to have hamburgers.
② I'm very glad to see you again.
③ To play computer games is exciting.
④ I need a magazine to read on the airplane.
⑤ He went to China to see the Great Wall of China.

21

> The windmill generated electricity by using the wind. She was amazed ⓐ to see that it worked quite well. She clapped her hands with joy.
> * windmill: 풍차

① I expect him to come early.
② She gave me a jacket to wear.
③ He was glad to be back in school.
④ My dream is to become an English teacher.
⑤ It is difficult to learn a foreign language.

22 서술형

표의 내용과 일치하도록 문장을 완성하시오.

오전	오후
feed the dog	take care of my brother

(1) Q1: What did your mom have you do in the morning?
A1: My mom ________________________.

(2) Q2: What did your mom ask you to do in the afternoon?
A2: My mom ________________________.

고난도

23 서술형

다음 조건에 맞춰 ⓐ를 영어로 바꿔 쓰시오.

조건
1. 괄호 안의 단어를 모두 사용할 것
2. 필요한 단어를 추가할 것
3.「It ~ to + 동사원형」 가주어 · 진주어 구문을 사용할 것

W: What does Kevin have to do to become a good singer?

M: ⓐ 연습을 가능한 한 많이 하는 것이 그에게 중요해. (practice, important, as, much, him, for)

→ It ______________________________
______________________________.

고난도

24 서술형

밑줄 친 부분이 어법에 맞으면 O, 맞지 않으면 바르게 고쳐 쓰시오.

(1) It is very nice for you to help me.
(2) It is natural of him to help the poor.
(3) It was careless of you to lose the wallet.
(4) It is possible of her to be the class president.
(5) It is so generous of you to offer us this opportunity.
(6) My teacher told us not to make noise during the class.

(1) → ______________________________
(2) → ______________________________
(3) → ______________________________
(4) → ______________________________
(5) → ______________________________
(6) → ______________________________

고난도

25 서술형 심화

그림을 보고, 대화의 흐름이 자연스럽도록 괄호 안의 말을 활용하여 빈칸에 알맞은 말을 쓰시오.

(1)

(2)

(3)

(1) A: What did Nick's mom ask Nick to do?
B: His mom ______________________________
______________. (wash, the dishes)

(2) B: Can you tell me ______________________________
______________________ from here? (how, the bank, get)
G: Sure. You can take bus Number 752.

(3) B: How was the English test?
G: It was ______________________________
______________ the questions. (difficult, me, answer)

CHAPTER 03

동명사

동명사

「동사원형 –ing」의 형태로, 동사의 성질을 가진 채로 문장 안에서 명사처럼 주어, 보어, 목적어의 역할을 한다. 동명사가 목적어의 역할을 할 때, 동사에 따라 동명사만을 목적어로 취하는 경우가 있다. 반면에 to부정사만을 목적어로 취하는 동사도 있으므로 주의해야 한다.

cf. 현재분사도 동명사처럼 「동사원형-ing」의 형태이지만, 현재분사는 문장에서 형용사 역할을 한다.

한눈에 쏙! 문법 Chart

<table>
<tr><td>동명사의 역할</td><td colspan="4">(1) 주어 역할 – 단수 취급
(2) 보어 역할
(3) 목적어 역할
(4) 전치사의 목적어</td></tr>
<tr><td>동명사의 의미상 주어</td><td colspan="4">대개 동명사 앞에 소유격이나 목적격을 써서 나타낸다.</td></tr>
<tr><td>동명사의 부정</td><td colspan="4">동명사 앞에 not 또는 never</td></tr>
<tr><td>동명사의 시제</td><td colspan="4">(1) 문장의 본동사와 동일한 시제일 때: 「동사원형–ing」
(2) 문장의 본동사보다 한 시제 앞설 때: 「having + p.p.」</td></tr>
<tr><td>동명사의 수동태</td><td colspan="4">(1) 문장의 본동사와 같은 시제이고 수동태일 때: 「being + p.p.」
(2) 문장의 본동사보다 한 시제 앞서고 수동태일 때: 「having + been + p.p.」</td></tr>
<tr><td>동명사를 목적어로 취하는 동사</td><td colspan="4">mind, enjoy, give up, avoid, finish, escape, practice, stop, consider 등
(to부정사를 목적어로 취하는 동사: want, expect, hope, wish, decide, plan, promise, refuse 등)</td></tr>
<tr><td rowspan="4">목적어의 형태에 따라 의미가 달라지는 동사들</td><td>remember + 동명사(-ing)</td><td>(과거)~했던 것을 기억하다</td><td>remember + to부정사</td><td>(미래)~할 것을 기억하다</td></tr>
<tr><td>forget + 동명사(-ing)</td><td>(과거)~했던 것을 잊다</td><td>forget + to부정사</td><td>(미래)~할 것을 잊다</td></tr>
<tr><td>try + 동명사(-ing)</td><td>(시도)시험 삼아 ~해 보다</td><td>try + to부정사</td><td>(노력)~하려고 애쓰다</td></tr>
<tr><td>regret + 동명사(-ing)</td><td>(과거)~했던 것을 후회하다</td><td>regret + to부정사</td><td>(미래)~하게 되어 유감이다</td></tr>
</table>

핵심만 쏙! 문법 Point

Point 01 동명사는 문장에서 명사처럼 쓰여요!

- **동명사**는 「**동사원형-ing**」의 형태로 문장에서 명사처럼 **주어**, **보어**, **목적어** 역할을 한다. 주어로 쓰인 동명사는 **단수 취급**한다.
  Reading one book a week is my goal. 일주일에 한 권씩 책을 읽는 것이 나의 목표이다. (주어)
  My volunteer work is helping handicapped people. 나의 봉사 활동은 장애우를 돕는 것이다. (보어)
- **동사의 목적어로 쓰이는 동명사**: 동사 **mind, enjoy, give up, avoid, finish, escape, practice, stop, consider** 등은 목적어로 동명사가 온다.
  He really enjoys **building** things with blocks. 그는 블록으로 무언가 만드는 것을 정말로 좋아한다.
- **전치사의 목적어로 쓰이는 동명사**: 전치사의 목적어로 동사(구)가 올 때에는 **동명사(동사원형-ing)** 형태로 온다. 이때 쓰인 동명사는 to부정사로 바꿔 쓸 수 없다.
  Jiho is interested in **representing** Korea. 지호는 한국을 대표하는 것에 관심이 있다.

Point 02 동명사의 의미상 주어는 동명사 앞에 소유격이나 목적격으로 써요!

- **동명사의 의미상의 주어**: 대개 **동명사 앞에 소유격**이나 **목적격**을 써서 나타낸다.
  Do you mind if I open the window? (open의 행위자가 I) 제가 창문을 좀 열어도 될까요?
  Do you mind my[me] opening the window? (문장의 주어 you ≠ 동명사의 행위자인 my/me)
- **동명사의 의미상의 주어를 생략하는 경우**: 동명사의 행위자가 문장의 주어, 목적어와 같거나 또는 일반적인 사람인 경우에는 의미상의 주어는 따로 명시하지 않고 생략한다.
  Do you mind opening the window? 창문을 좀 열어 주시겠어요? (문장의 주어 you = 동명사의 행위자)
  Thank you for telling me the truth. 진실을 말해주셔서 고맙습니다. (문장의 목적어 you = 동명사의 행위자)
  Getting up late is a bad habit. 늦게 일어나는 것은 나쁜 습관이다. (일반적인 사람들 = 동명사의 행위자)
- **동명사의 부정**: **동명사 앞에 not 또는 never**를 쓴다.
  Mom was angry at me for not coming back home earlier.
  엄마는 내가 더 일찍 집에 돌아오지 않아서 화가 나셨다.

Point 03 주절의 시제보다 먼저 일어난 동작의 동명사는 완료형으로 써요!

- **동명사의 시제 표현**
  (1) **문장의 본동사와 동일한 시제일 때**: 「동사원형-ing」
  I don't mind sharing the table. = I don't mind that I share the table.
  (2) **문장의 본동사보다 한 시제 앞설 때**: 「having + p.p.」
  John is proud of having got an A in math. = John is proud that he got an A in math.
- **동명사의 수동태**
  (1) **문장의 본동사와 같은 시제이고 수동태일 때**: 「being + p.p.」
  He doesn't like being treated as a little kid. 그는 어린아이로 취급 받는 것을 좋아하지 않는다.
  (2) **문장의 본동사보다 한 시제 앞서고 수동태일 때**: 「having + been + p.p.」
  She felt honored by having been elected as the school president.
  그녀는 학생회장으로 선출된 것을 영광으로 여겼다.

핵심만 콕! 문법 Check

A 괄호 안에서 알맞은 말을 모두 고르시오.

1 Keeping secrets (is, are) very important.
2 (Being, To be, Be) a good friend means being a good listener.
3 Their job is (correcting, to correct, correct) wrong information about Korea.
4 Hojun enjoys (working, to work) on his blog.
5 Thank you for (inviting, to invite, invite) me to the party.
6 Do you mind (I, my, me) taking a picture of you?
7 I am worried about (she, her) being disappointed.

B 밑줄 친 부분이 어법에 맞으면 O표, 틀리면 바르게 고쳐 쓰시오.

1 She is good at <u>designing</u> web pages. → ______________
2 She tried to avoid <u>to meet</u> him today. → ______________
3 Bill is thinking of <u>make</u> a robot. → ______________
4 I am sure of <u>not his cleaning</u> his car tomorrow. → ______________

C 우리말과 뜻이 같도록 괄호 안의 말을 바르게 배열하여 문장을 완성하시오.

1 그녀는 수업에 늦을까 봐 걱정했다. (be late)
→ She was afraid of ________ ________ for the class.

2 엄마는 내가 숙제를 끝낸 후에 나가도록 허락해 주셨다. (do)
→ Mom allowed me to go out after I finished ________ my homework.

3 나는 그 때 그녀가 아팠던 것을 알아채지 못했다. (be)
→ I wasn't aware of ________ ________ sick at that time.

4 그녀는 자신이 좋아하는 TV 프로그램을 놓치지 않게 되어서 기뻤다. (miss)
→ She was happy about ________ ________ her favorite TV show.

5 엄마는 내가 경기를 포기해서 실망하셨다. (give up)
→ Mom is disappointed by ________ ________ ________ up the competition.

핵심만 쏙! 문법 Point

Point 04 동사의 종류에 따라 목적어의 형태가 달라져요!

- **동명사만을 목적어로 취하는 동사**

mind, enjoy, give up, avoid, finish, escape, practice, stop, consider 등	+	동명사

I finished writing the essay. 나는 그 과제물 쓰는 것을 끝마쳤다.

- **to부정사만을 목적어로 취하는 동사**

want, expect, hope, wish, decide, plan, promise, refuse 등	+	to부정사

We all hope to achieve success in the future. 우리는 모두 미래에 성공을 성취하기를 바란다.

- 동명사와 to부정사 둘 다 목적어로 취하는 동사들이 있다.

(1) **의미상 차이가 없는 경우**: 동사 **start, begin, like, love, hate, continue** 등은 별다른 **의미 차이 없이 to부정사와 동명사를 모두 목적어로** 취한다.
She hates fighting with her friends. = She hates to fight with her friends.

(2) **의미상 차이가 있는 경우**: to부정사와 동명사를 모두 목적어로 취하지만 **의미가 달라지는 동사들**은 다음과 같다.

remember + 동명사(-ing)	(과거) ~했던 것을 기억하다	remember + to부정사	(미래) ~할 것을 기억하다
forget + 동명사(-ing)	(과거) ~했던 것을 잊다	forget + to부정사	(미래) ~할 것을 잊다
try + 동명사(-ing)	(시도) 시험 삼아 ~해 보다	try + to부정사	(노력) ~하려고 애쓰다
regret + 동명사(-ing)	(과거) ~했던 것을 후회하다	regret + to부정사	(미래) ~하게 되어 유감이다

She forgot to turn off the light. 그녀는 불을 끄는 것을 잊었다. (→ 불을 끄지 않았음)
She forgot turning off the light. 그녀는 불을 끈 사실을 잊었다. (→ 불을 껐음)

Point 05 동명사는 명사처럼, 현재분사는 형용사처럼 쓰여요!

- 동명사와 현재분사는 둘 다 형태는 「동사원형-ing」이다. 하지만, **동명사**는 명사처럼 문장에서 **주어, 보어, 목적어의 역할**을 하고, **현재분사**는 **형용사처럼 명사를 수식**하거나 **보어**로 쓰인다.

His dream was climbing Mt. Everest. (보어: 동명사 – '~하기(하는 것)'으로 해석됨)
The girl was smiling at him. (보어: 현재분사 – '~하고 있는'으로 해석됨)
※ 「동사~ing」가 명사 앞에서 수식할 때, 수식받는 명사의 "목적, 용도"를 나타내면 동명사, "상태"를 나타내면 현재분사이다.

Point 06 자주 쓰이는 동명사 표현은 꼭 외워둡시다!

look forward to -ing	~할 것을 고대하다	go -ing	~하러 가다
How[What] about -ing?	~하는 게 어때?	spend *A* (on) -ing	~하는 데 *A*를 쓰다
be used to -ing	~하는 데에 익숙하다	be busy -ing	~하느라 바쁘다
can't help -ing	~하지 않을 수 없다	have trouble -ing	~하는데 어려움을 겪다
keep[stop] *A* from -ing	*A*를 ~못하게 하다	feel like -ing	~하고 싶다
there is no -ing	~은 불가능하다	on -ing	~하자마자
It is no use -ing	~해도 소용없다	be worth -ing	~할 가치가 있다

핵심만 콕! 문법 Check

A 괄호 안에서 알맞은 말을 고르시오.

1 Father promised (stopping, to stop) smoking.
2 She didn't mind (waiting, to wait) for more time.
3 They planned (going, to go) hiking this weekend.
4 Jason has practiced (playing, to play) soccer for more than two years.
5 Susan stopped (talking, to talk) over the phone to hear the sound from outside.
6 She tried (opening, to open) the bottle cap, but she couldn't.
7 Please remember (buying, to buy) some ice cream on the way home.
8 She stopped (drinking, to drink) coffee in the late afternoon for a good night sleep.
9 Mom forgot (leaving, to leave) her wallet in her car and looked for it in the house.

B 밑줄 친 부분이 어법에 맞으면 O표, 틀리면 바르게 고쳐 쓰시오.

1 Yumi never gave up pursuing her dream. → ______
2 Junho hoped visiting his cousin in China. → ______
3 Jane considers becoming a nurse in the future. → ______
4 She didn't really enjoy to listen to the rock music. → ______
5 How about study in the library for the exam? → ______
6 They couldn't help to laugh at the funny sight. → ______
7 She had trouble to find information on the Internet. → ______

C 우리말과 뜻이 같도록 괄호 안의 말을 바르게 배열하여 문장을 완성하시오.

1 그는 주말에 등반하는 것을 매우 좋아한다. (climbing, loves)
→ He ______ the mountain on weekends.

2 Jake는 자신의 사업을 시작하기를 원하고 있다. (wants, start, to)
→ Jake ______ his own business.

3 그들은 놀이공원에 가는 것을 고대하고 있다. (going, forward, to, looking)
→ They are ______ to the amusement park.

4 엎질러진 우유를 두고 울어 봐야 소용없다. (이미 엎질러진 물이다.) (no, use, crying, is)
→ It ______ over spilt milk.

내신 만점! 실전 기출

[1~2] 빈칸에 알맞은 말을 고르시오.

01

She enjoys ________ a diary in English.

① to keep ② keeping
③ kept ④ to keeping
⑤ keep

02

Mina was interested in ________ Italian cooking.

① learn ② learns
③ learning ④ learned
⑤ to learn

[3~4] 빈칸에 알맞지 않은 것을 고르시오.

03

We were all surprised at ________ giving up the competition.

① he ② his
③ her ④ them
⑤ their

04

She ________ searching for information on the Internet.

① began ② started
③ stopped ④ decided
⑤ kept

[5~7] 우리말과 뜻이 같도록 빈칸에 알맞은 말을 고르시오.

05

그녀는 불을 끄는 것을 잊어버렸다.
→ She forgot ________ off the light.

① turned ② turning
③ turn ④ to turn
⑤ turns

06

그는 집에 가는 길에 세탁소에서 옷을 가져가야 하는 것을 기억하고 있었다.
→ He remembered ________ up his clothes from the laundry on the way home.

① picked ② picking
③ pick ④ to pick
⑤ picks

07

그들은 숙제를 제 시간에 끝내기 위해 노력했다.
→ They tried ________ their homework on time.

① finish ② finishing
③ finished ④ to finish
⑤ to finishing

08 서술형

괄호 안의 말을 빈칸에 알맞은 형태로 바꿔 쓰시오.

나의 개는 나와 산책하는 것을 고대하고 있다. (take)

→ My dog is ________ ________ ________ ________ a walk with me.

[09~10] 밑줄 친 부분의 쓰임이 나머지와 다른 것을 고르시오.

09

① Visiting Jeju Island with you was very fun.
② Lots of fish are dying because of pollution.
③ He is interested in saving the environment.
④ His goal is going forward one step at a time.
⑤ She regretted telling her secret to Jenny yesterday.

10

① That <u>sleeping</u> baby in the cradle is so cute!
② There were some people in the <u>waiting</u> room.
③ The <u>dancing</u> girls in his picture all look beautiful.
④ Swamps are good places to live for many <u>living</u> creatures.
⑤ The <u>leaning</u> tower of Pisa is a famous tourist attraction in Italy.

11 어법상 옳은 문장은?

① Mothers never stop loving their children.
② They decided saving money to buy a new car.
③ Develop a good habit takes a lot of time and effort.
④ She didn't mind to leave her bag in the waiting room.
⑤ Don't forget buying some ice cream when you come back.

12 어법상 <u>어색한</u> 문장은?

① How about taking a break for a minute?
② Global warming is a result of increasing CO_2.
③ Some people wanted to take pictures of themselves.
④ The quiz show host started asking questions of the participants.
⑤ Remember calling me right after you wake up tomorrow morning.

[13~14] 두 문장의 뜻이 같도록 빈칸에 알맞은 말을 쓰시오.

13 서술형

Captain Jack is worried that he might not find the treasure.

→ Captain Jack is worried about ________ ________ the treasure.

14 서술형

I am sorry that I missed the first part of the movie.

→ I am sorry for ________ ________ the first part of the movie.

15 빈칸 ⓐ~ⓑ에 알맞은 말이 순서대로 바르게 나열된 것은?

- On ⓐ ________ home, Peter turned on his computer to check the email from Sally.
- My mom is used to ⓑ ________ up early in the morning.

① return, get
② returns, gets
③ returning, got
④ returning, getting
⑤ returned, getting

16 대화의 흐름이 자연스럽도록 빈칸에 알맞은 말을 <u>모두</u> 고르면?

A: Did you send your book report via e-mail? I didn't receive it yet.
B: I'm sorry. ________________.

① I forgot sending the e-mail.
② I forgot to send the e-mail.
③ I had trouble sending the e-mail.
④ I was very busy sending the e-mail.
⑤ I'm looking forward to sending the e-mail.

[17~18] 어법상 어색한 부분을 찾아 바르게 고쳐 쓰시오.

17 서술형

사서는 아이들이 도서관에서 떠들지 못하도록 했다.
→ The librarian kept children in making noise in the library.

__________ → __________

18 서술형

Mike는 아빠와 함께 주말에 낚시 가는 것을 매우 좋아한다.
→ Mike likes going to fish on weekends with his father.

__________ → __________

19 ⓐ~ⓔ의 어법에 대한 설명 중 옳은 것은?

Jenny is going to give a presentation about the environment tomorrow. She is planning ⓐ to talk about ways of ⓑ help the environment. She is interested in ⓒ saving the planet. She remembers ⓓ to watch a documentary about sea animals dying because of an oil spill the other day. She thinks that ⓔ to show the video clip in her presentation will be very helpful.

① ⓐ는 어법상 어색한 부분이 있다.
② ⓑ는 to help로 바꾸어야 한다.
③ ⓒ는 save로 바꾸어 써야 한다.
④ ⓓ는 어법상 어색한 부분이 없다.
⑤ ⓔ는 showing으로도 쓸 수 있다.

20 서술형

괄호 안의 말을 활용하여 ⓐ를 영어로 옮길 때 빈칸에 알맞은 말을 쓰시오.

A: You look upset. What's wrong?
B: ⓐ 나는 매일 똑같은 교복을 입는 것이 싫증이 나. (get tired of, wear)

→ I am ________ ________ ________ ________ the same uniform every day.

[21~22] 다음을 읽고 물음에 답하시오.

Jisu: ⓐ Thank you for inviting me to this concert. ⓑ I have been looking forward to see it for a long time!
Minho: Really? I am happy to hear that.
Jisu: ⓒ I spent almost an hour to buy tickets but I couldn't get any.
Minho: I know. ⓓ I also had trouble getting tickets myself at first. These guys are really popular!
Jisu: They really are! Can we go a little closer to the stage? ⓔ The tall guys in front of us keep block my sight.
Minho: ⓕ It seems that there is no getting any closer to the stage because there are so many people.
Jisu: Oh! What a pity!

신유형

21 위 대화문의 내용을 잘못 이해한 학생은?

① 민지: 민호가 지수를 콘서트에 데리고 갔구나.
② 수지: 지수는 오랫동안 이 콘서트를 기다려 왔어.
③ 찬호: 지수는 표를 구하려고 했지만 사지 못했어.
④ 희진: 지수의 자리에서 무대가 아주 잘 보여.
⑤ 진수: 사람들이 많아서 두 사람이 무대 쪽으로 더 가까이 가는 것은 불가능해.

최다빈출

22 위 글의 ⓐ~ⓕ 중 어법상 틀린 문장을 모두 고르면?

① ⓐ, ⓒ, ⓔ ② ⓑ, ⓓ, ⓕ
③ ⓐ, ⓓ, ⓔ ④ ⓑ, ⓔ, ⓕ
⑤ ⓑ, ⓒ, ⓔ

23 어법상 옳은 문장을 모두 고르면?

ⓐ John will finish building a robot soon.
ⓑ He never gave up to look for his lost dog.
ⓒ His not obeying the rules can get him into trouble.
ⓓ Please stop to talk as the movie is going to start now.
ⓔ They have been practicing singing for more than a month.
ⓕ Jerry was ashamed of he making a mistake in the competition.

① 1개 ② 2개 ③ 3개 ④ 4개 ⑤ 5개

24 서술형

우리말과 일치하도록 괄호 안의 말을 바르게 배열하여 문장을 완성하시오. (단, 필요하면 주어진 단어의 형태를 변화시킬 것)

자신이 어떻게 보이는지에 신경을 쓰는 것이 학생들에게 너무 큰 관심거리가 되어서는 안 된다.
(care, about, look, how, they)

→ ____________ ____________ ____________
____________ ____________ should not be
a big interest for children.

고난도

25 서술형 심화

그림을 보고 괄호 안의 말을 활용하여, 수업 시간의 규칙에 관한 문장을 완성하시오.

(1)

(raise your hand)

(2)

(use a cell phone)

(3)

(talk with your friends)

Class Rules

(1) Please remember ____________
____________ ____________ ____________
if you have a question.

(2) ____________ ____________ ____________
____________ is not allowed.

(3) Avoid ____________ ____________
____________ ____________.

CHAPTER 04

분사

분사

동사의 형태를 변화시켜 형용사처럼 쓰는 것을 분사라고 한다. 또한 진행형, 수동태, 완료형 문장을 만들 때에도 분사를 쓴다. 분사에는 현재분사와 과거분사가 있는데, 현재분사는 「동사원형-ing」형태로 능동, 진행의 의미를 나타내고, 과거분사는 대개 「동사원형-ed」의 형태로 수동, 완료의 의미를 나타낸다.

한눈에 쏙! 문법 Chart

• 현재분사 *vs.* 과거분사

	현재분사	과거분사
형태	동사원형-ing	동사원형-(e)d 또는 불규칙한 형태
의미	능동(~하는), 진행(~하고 있는 중인)	수동(~된 , ~당한), 완료(~한)
감정을 나타낼 때	분사가 수식하는 명사가 감정을 유발하는 원인인 경우 I heard the **surprising** news last night.	분사가 수식하는 명사가 감정을 느끼는 주체 We were **surprised** by the news.
분사구문 만드는 법	① 부사절의 접속사 생략한다. ② 부사절의 주어가 주절의 주어와 같으면 생략, 다르면 남긴다. ③ 부사절의 시제가 주절의 시제와 같으면 { 동사를 –ing형태로 쓰고, 앞서면 부사절의 동사를 having + p.p.로 쓴다. ④ 「being/having been + 분사」의 형태일 때는 being/having been을 생략한다.	
부대상황	with + 명사 + { 현재분사 (명사와 분사가 능동관계) / 과거분사 (명사와 분사가 수동관계)	

핵심만 쏙! 문법 Point

Point 01 현재분사(동사원형-ing)는 능동(~하는)이나 진행(~하고 있는)의 의미를 나타내요!

The singing boy is my younger brother. 노래하고 있는 그 소년이 나의 남동생이다. (명사 수식)

They are looking at the posters on the wall. 그들은 벽에 붙은 포스터를 보고 있다. (진행)

Point 02 과거분사(동사원형-ed)는 수동(~된, ~당한)이나 완료(~한, ~해 온)의 의미를 나타내요!

We found the broken window. 우리는 깨진 창문을 발견했다. (명사 수식)

His book will be published next year. 그의 책은 내년에 출간될 것이다. (수동태)
I have already seen those movies many times. 나는 그 영화들을 이미 여러 번 보았다. (완료)

Point 03 분사는 형용사처럼 명사를 수식하거나 보어의 역할을 해요!

- **명사를 수식 (한정적 용법)**: 분사 단독으로 명사를 수식할 때에는 명사의 앞에서, 분사가 구를 이루어 명사를 수식할 때에는 명사의 뒤에서 꾸며준다.
  I heard the surprising news about him. 나는 그에 대한 놀라운 소식을 들었다. (명사 앞에서 수식)

  I received an e-mail written in English. 나는 영어로 쓰인 이메일을 받았다. (명사 뒤에서 수식)

- **보어 역할 (서술적 용법)**: 분사가 주어나 목적어를 보충 설명해 주는 보어 역할을 할 수 있다.
  She looked excited when she heard the news. 그녀는 소식을 들었을 때 신이 나 보였다. (주격 보어)
  I found the book very interesting. 나는 그 책이 매우 재미있다는 것을 알았다. (목적격 보어)

Point 04 감정을 유발할 때는 현재분사(-ing), 감정을 느낄 때는 과거분사(-ed)를 써요!

- 분사가 직접 수식하거나 보충 설명하는 명사가 감정을 유발하는 원인일 경우에는 **현재분사(동사원형-ing)**를 쓰고, 감정을 느끼는 주체일 경우에는 **과거분사(동사원형-ed)**를 쓴다.

현재분사 (~한 감정을 느끼게 하는)	과거분사 (~한 감정을 느끼는)
amazing 놀라운	amazed 놀란
confusing 혼란스럽게 하는	confused 혼란스러운
depressing 우울하게 하는	depressed 우울한
fascinating 매혹적인	fascinated 매료된
frightening 깜짝 놀라게 하는	frightened 깜짝 놀란
disappointing 실망시키는	disappointed 실망한
moving 감동적인	moved 감동한
satisfying 만족스러운	satisfied 만족해하는

His speech for the graduates was amazing. 졸업생들을 위한 그의 강연은 놀라웠다. (현재분사)
Many graduates were amazed by his speech. 많은 졸업생들은 그의 강연에 놀랐다. (과거분사)

핵심만 콕! 문법 Check

A 괄호 안에서 알맞은 말을 고르시오.

1 The price of gold is (rising, risen) these days.
2 Our lives are (filling, filled) with a lot of things to do.
3 The watches (making, made) in Switzerland are popular.
4 They have been (playing, played) games for two hours.

B 밑줄 친 부분이 어법에 맞으면 O표, 틀리면 바르게 고쳐 쓰시오.

1 I think my wallet was <u>stealing</u>. → ______________
2 The dishes were <u>broken</u> by Tom. → ______________
3 Her parents were <u>pleasing</u> with the result. → ______________
4 Look at the beautiful girl <u>written</u> a letter. → ______________

C 괄호 안의 말을 빈칸에 알맞은 형태로 쓰시오.

1 I think she has a ______________ voice. (fascinate)
2 She was ______________ and not sure what to do. (confuse)
3 People were ______________ by the beautiful story. (touch)
4 Most of the audience were ______________ with the play. (bore)

D 우리말과 뜻이 같도록 괄호 안의 말을 바르게 배열하여 문장을 완성하시오.

1 나는 이 작가에 의해 집필된 공상 과학 소설들을 좋아한다. (novels, this, written, author, by)
→ I like the science fiction ______________________________.

2 너는 우리 선생님으로부터 그 놀라운 소식을 들었니? (shocking, from, the, our, teacher, news)
→ Did you hear ______________________________?

3 그 레스토랑은 항상 많은 방문객들로 붐빈다. (always, with, crowded, visitors, many)
→ The restaurant is ______________________________.

핵심만 쏙! 문법 Point

Point 05 분사구문을 만들 때는 ①접속사 생략 가능 + ②주어 생략 + ③동사원형 + ing!

- 분사구문을 만드는 법
  ① 부사절의 접속사를 생략한다. (뜻을 명확하게 강조하고 싶을 경우, 남겨 둘 수도 있다.)
  ② 주절의 주어와 부사절의 주어가 같으면 부사절의 주어를 생략하고, 다르면 남긴다.
  ③ 부사절의 동사를 현재분사 형태로 바꾼다.
  As she was exhausted, Julie decided to go home early.
  ① ② ③
  → (Being) exhausted, Julie decided to go home early. Julie는 기진맥진해서 집에 일찍 가기로 결정했다.

  ※ 단, 부사절의 시제가 주절의 시제보다 이전인 경우, 부사절의 동사를 「having + p.p.」 형태로 쓴다.
  After he had finished his homework, he went to bed.
  → Having finished his homework, he went to bed. 숙제를 마친 후에, 그는 잠자리에 들었다.

  ※ 분사구문이 Being 또는 Having been으로 시작할 경우, Being 또는 Having been은 생략 가능하다.

  ※ 분사구문의 부정: 분사 앞에 not이나 never를 쓴다. (☞ p. 44의 Point 9참고)

Point 06 부사절의 시제가 주절의 시제보다 이전인 경우, 「having + 과거분사(p.p.)」을 써요!

- As he had read the book before, he didn't want to read it again.
  → Having read the book before, he didn't want to read it again.
  그는 전에 그 책을 읽은 적이 있었기 때문에, 그 책을 다시 읽기를 원하지 않았다.
  Since she lived in England when she was young, her English is good.
  → Having lived in England when she was young, her English is good.
  어릴 때 영국에 살았기 때문에 그녀의 영어는 유창하다.

Point 07 「Being + 과거분사(p.p.)」와 「Having been + 과거분사(p.p.)」에서 being 또는 having been은 생략할 수 있어요!

- (Being) Elected as the school president, he was very happy.
  학교 회장으로 선출되어서 그는 매우 기뻤다.
  (Having been) Repaired by my Dad, the car worked well.
  나의 아버지에 의해 수리되고 나서, 그 차는 잘 작동했다.

Point 08 분사구문에는 부대상황, 시간, 이유/원인 등의 뜻이 있어요!

- Raising his hand, the boy stood up. (= The boy raised his hand and stood up.) 〈부대상황: while, as〉
  Looking at the calendar, he realized it was his mom's birthday. 〈시간: when, while, after, before등〉
  (= When he looked at the calendar, he realized it was his mom's birthday.)
  Wanting to stay alone, she didn't make an appointment with her friend. 〈이유/원인: as, because, since〉
  (= Because she wanted to stay alone, she didn't make an appointment with her friend.)

핵심만 콕! 문법 Check

A 두 문장의 뜻이 같도록 분사구문을 활용하여 바꿔 쓰시오.

1 When you spend money, you have to think twice.
→ When ______________________, you have to think twice.

2 Because Sally had studied hard, she got a scholarship.
→ ______________________, Sally got a scholarship.

B 두 문장의 뜻이 같도록 빈칸에 알맞은 말을 〈보기〉에서 골라 쓰시오.

보기		
because	because of	after

1 Having nothing to eat, he decided to cook himself dinner.
→ ____________ he had nothing to eat, he decided to cook himself dinner.

2 Graduating from school, I got a job in this company.
→ ____________ I graduated from school, I got a job in this company.

C 우리말과 뜻이 같도록 빈칸에 생략된 being 또는 having been을 써 넣으시오.

1 그는 천재이기 때문에, 항상 만점을 받는다.
→ ______________ a genius, he always gets a perfect score.

2 그녀는 프랑스에서 자랐기 때문에 프랑스어를 매우 잘할 수 있다.
→ ______________ raised in France, she can speak French very well.

D 밑줄 친 부분을 분사구문으로 바꿔 쓰시오.

1 <u>Since she had spent all her money</u>, she couldn't buy new clothes.
→ ______________________, she couldn't buy new clothes.

2 <u>Because he had been impressed by her music</u>, he became her fan.
→ ______________________, he became her fan.

3 <u>As he had got a good score on the test</u>, Tim could enter a good university.
→ ______________________, Tim could enter a good university.

핵심만 쏙! 문법 Point

Point 09 분사구문을 부정할 때는 분사 앞에 not이나 never를 붙여요!

- Not knowing what to do next, she asked for his help.
  (= As she didn't know what to do next, she asked for his help.)
  다음에 무엇을 할지 몰라서 그녀는 그의 도움을 요청했다.
  Not having read the magazine, I couldn't tell you about it.
  (= As I hadn't read the magazine, I couldn't tell you about it.)
  내가 그 잡지를 읽지 않았기 때문에, 그것에 대해 네게 이야기 해 줄 수 없었다.

Point 10 분사구문의 의미를 명확히 전달하기 위해 접속사를 남겨두기도 해요!

- After talking to her, I always feel better. 그녀와 이야기를 하고 나면, 나는 항상 기분이 나아진다.
  (= After I talk to her, I always feel better.)

Point 11 주절과 종속절의 주어가 서로 다른 경우, 분사구문에서 주어를 생략하지 않아요!

- It being a fine day, we decided to go on a picnic. 날씨가 좋아서 우리는 소풍을 가기로 했다.
  (= As it was a fine day, we decided to go on a picnic.)

Point 12 「with +명사+분사」구문: '~을 한 채로'라는 뜻으로, 부대상황이나 동시 동작을 나타내요!

with + 명사 + 현재분사	명사와 분사가 능동 관계	She smiled with tears running down her cheek. 그녀는 뺨에 눈물이 흘러내리는 채로 웃었다.
with + 명사 + 과거분사	명사와 분사가 수동 관계	He is standing with his arms folded. 그는 팔짱을 낀 채로 서 있다.

Point 13 분사구문의 주어가 일반인일 때 주어를 굳이 밝히지 않고 생략해요!

Generally speaking 일반적으로 말해서 Frankly speaking 솔직히 말해서 Strictly speaking 엄밀히 말해서 Speaking of ~에 대해 말하자면	Considering ~을 고려하자면 Judging from ~로 판단하건대 Compared with ~와 비교해보면

Speaking of the holiday, have you made any plans yet? 휴가에 대해 말하니 말인데, 어떤 계획이라도 세웠니?
Considering his age, his writing skill is amazing. 그의 나이를 고려하건대, 그의 작문 실력은 대단하다.

핵심만 콕! 문법 Check

A 밑줄 친 부분에서 어법상 틀린 부분을 한 군데 찾아 바르게 고쳐 쓰시오.

1 There being many people, we had to wait for an hour.
→ As there being many people, we had to wait for an hour.
______________ → ______________

2 Not having seen each other for a few months, they missed each other.
→ Because they had seen each other for a few months, they missed each other.
______________ → ______________

B 다음 문장과 같은 뜻이 되도록 분사구문을 이용하여 바꿔 쓰시오.

1 Because I didn't feel hungry, I skipped my lunch.
→ ______________________, I skipped my lunch.

2 Because there was no bus so late at night, he had to take a taxi.
→ ______________________, he had to take a taxi.

C 두 문장의 뜻이 같도록 「with + 명사 + 분사」구문을 활용하여 문장을 완성하시오.

1 The man was listening to music, and his eyes were closed.
→ The man was listening to music ______________________.

2 The man is deep in thought, and his arms are folded.
→ The man is deep in thought ______________________.

D 우리말과 뜻이 같도록 괄호 안의 말을 활용하여 문장을 완성하시오.

1 그의 억양으로 판단하건대 그는 영국 출신이다. (judge)
→ ____________ ____________ his accent, he is from England.

2 솔직히 말하자면, 나는 기분이 상했다. (frankly)
→ ____________ ____________, I felt upset.

내신 만점! 실전 기출

01 빈칸에 알맞은 말이 순서대로 바르게 나열된 것은?

- Be careful of the __________ glass on the floor.
- Do you know the boy __________ next to Linda?

① break, sit
② broke, sat
③ broken, sitting
④ breaking, to sit
⑤ to break, is sitting

02 서술형

괄호 안의 말을 바르게 배열하여 문장을 완성하시오.

A: Where is your uncle?
B: He's over there. ______________ is my uncle. (man, the, a wheelchair, riding)

→ ______________________________

____

03 밑줄 친 부분이 어법에 맞지 않는 것은?

① Look at the girl singing on the stage.
② The boy played on the ground is John.
③ The poem written by Sue was very touching.
④ The people invited to the party didn't show up.
⑤ Movies directed by Christopher Nolan are always amazing.

04 밑줄 친 부분을 분사구문을 활용하여 바르게 바꿔 쓴 문장을 고르시오.

As I knew it was my fault, I sincerely apologized.

① Know my fault, I sincerely apologized.
② Known my fault, I sincerely apologized.
③ As my fault, I sincerely apologized.
④ Knowing it was my fault, I sincerely apologized.
⑤ Having known it was my fault, I sincerely apologized.

05 밑줄 친 부분을 분사구문을 활용하여 바르게 바꿔 쓴 문장을 고르시오.

Because life is very short, we have to do what we like to do.

① Life is very short, we have to do what we like to do.
② Being very short, we have to do what we like to do.
③ Life being very short, we have to do what we like to do.
④ Because life very short, we have to do what we like to do.
⑤ Life having been very short, we have to do what we like to do.

06 서술형

다음을 한 문장으로 바꿔 쓸 때 빈칸에 알맞은 말을 쓰시오.

I saw a huge trailer. It was blocking the narrow road to my house.

→ I saw a huge trailer ______________________________

______________________________.

07 두 문장의 뜻이 같도록 빈칸에 알맞은 말을 고르시오.

As he was raised by his grandmother, he is very close to her.
= __________ raised by his grandmother, he is very close to her.

① Being
② Been
③ Having been
④ Was
⑤ He

최다빈출

[8~9] 어법에 맞지 않는 문장을 고르시오.

08

① My father loves to eat frozen yogurt.
② The songs performed last night were really nice.
③ The boy carried a box is our class president.
④ The mountain covered with snow was really beautiful.
⑤ I was very frightened to see a big dog on my way home.

09

① Not feeling well, he went straight back home.
② Exhausted, she fell asleep right after she came home.
③ Not being rich, she couldn't buy the watch.
④ Admitted what he did was wrong, he said he was sorry.
⑤ While waiting for my turn, I had a chat with other people.

고난도

10 다음을 분사구문이 포함된 문장으로 바르게 바꿔 쓴 것을 모두 고르면?

Because I was born and raised in a cold city, I am used to the cold.

① Being born and raised in a cold city, I am used to the cold.
② Born and raised in a cold city, I am used to the cold.
③ Was born and raised in a cold city, I am used to the cold.
④ Having been born and raised in a cold city, I am used to the cold.
⑤ Because being born and raised in a cold city, I am used to the cold.

11 빈칸 ⓐ, ⓑ에 알맞은 말이 순서대로 바르게 나열된 것은?

딸은 큰 가방을 들고 있는 아빠를 따라 밖으로 나왔다.
→ The daughter went out, ⓐ __________ her dad ⓑ __________ a big bag.

① follow, carry
② following, carrying
③ following, carried
④ followed, carrying
⑤ followed, carried

12 서술형

다음을 분사구문이 포함된 문장으로 바꿔 쓸 때 빈칸에 알맞은 말을 쓰시오.

Because I had not brought my wallet, I didn't have money to buy lunch.

→ ______________________________, I didn't have money to buy lunch.

13 빈칸에 공통으로 알맞은 말은?

- He was sitting under the tree __________ his cat sleeping near him.
- I don't think it's good to study __________ the music turned on.
- The boy was standing __________ his back leaning against the wall.

① on ② at ③ for
④ with ⑤ by

14 서술형

밑줄 친 부분을 괄호 안의 단어를 활용하여 절로 바꿔 쓰시오.

<u>She having many friends</u>, her school life is not lonely anymore. (Because)

→ ______________________________, her school life is not lonely anymore.

15 서술형

두 문장의 뜻이 같도록 분사구문을 활용하여 문장을 완성하시오.

> Because I didn't know how to solve the problem, I asked my sister for help.

→ ______________________________,
I asked my sister for help.

신유형

16 다음을 분사구문이 포함된 문장으로 만들 때, 어법상 틀린 부분을 찾아 바르게 고친 사람은?

> Because Junsu had lost his wallet, we had to buy him lunch.
> → ⓐ Because ⓑ Junsu ⓒ having been lost his wallet, ⓓ we had to buy him lunch.

① 민호: ⓐ Because를 꼭 생략해야 해.
② 지나: ⓑ Junsu를 생략해야 해.
③ 수지: ⓒ having been lost를 losing으로 바꿔야 해.
④ 예나: ⓒ having been lost를 having lost로 바꿔야 해.
⑤ 준호: ⓓ we를 he로 바꿔야 해.

17 밑줄 친 동사를 어법에 맞는 형태로 바꿔 순서대로 나열한 것은?

> A: Jenny, what do you like to do to relax?
> B: Well, I like to listen to music with my eyes close. It is really relax. How about you?
> A: I like to take a bath. It helps me to relieve my stress.

① closing, relax ② closing, relaxing
③ closed, relaxing ④ closed, relaxed
⑤ close, relaxed

18 다음 문장의 분사구문을 부사절로 바꿀 때 빈칸에 알맞은 말을 모두 고르면?

> Being good at speaking English, he could make foreign friends easily.
> → ______________________________,
> he could make foreign friends easily.

① Though he was good at speaking English
② Because he was good at speaking English
③ Although he was good at speaking English
④ Since he was good at speaking English
⑤ Unless he was good at speaking English

19 빈칸 ⓐ, ⓑ에 알맞은 말이 순서대로 바르게 나열된 것은?

> A: Hey. What's bothering you?
> B: I am reading an email ⓐ __________ in English. But I can't understand it perfectly. Some of the words are very ⓑ __________.
> A: Let me have a look. I think I can help you.

① writing, confusing ② writing, confused
③ written, confusing ④ written, confused
⑤ written, confuse

20 밑줄 친 부분을 부사절로 바꿔 쓸 때 빈칸에 알맞은 말은?

> Not having met for ages, we had many things to catch up on.
> → As we __________ for ages, we had many things to catch up on.

① didn't meet ② didn't have met
③ have not met ④ had not met
⑤ couldn't meet

21 밑줄 친 부분이 어법상 틀린 것은?

① He left the room with the radio turned on.
② I was lying on my back with my knees bending.
③ The man was sitting on a sofa with his legs crossed.
④ She told the story with tears rolling down her face.
⑤ Kevin was reading a newspaper with his wife knitting a sweater.

고난도

22 서술형

다음 ⓐ~ⓑ 중에서 어법상 어색한 부분을 한 군데 찾아 바르게 고쳐 쓰시오. (단, 분사구문을 유지/활용할 것)

ⓐ Surrounded by the sea, my hometown has many beautiful beaches.
ⓑ There was no one around me, I couldn't ask for help.

→ 기호: ________

____

____

고난도

23 다음 ⓐ~ⓒ에 알맞은 말이 순서대로 바르게 짝지어진 것은?

Last weekend, my friends and I visited a local hospital to do some volunteer work. In the hospital, I saw a little girl helping patients and ⓐ (smiling, smiled) beautifully to everyone. She looked like a volunteer like us. Soon, we became friends and I heard the ⓑ (surprising, surprised) news about her. She said she used to suffer from cancer and decided to help patients regularly after she had recovered. I was deeply ⓒ (impressed, impressing) with her story.

	ⓐ		ⓑ		ⓒ
①	smiled	—	surprising	—	impressing
②	smiling	—	surprised	—	impressing
③	smiled	—	surprising	—	impressed
④	smiling	—	surprised	—	impressed
⑤	smiling	—	surprising	—	impressed

24 서술형

〈보기〉와 같이, 우리말과 일치하도록 괄호 안의 말과 「with + 명사 + 분사」구문을 활용하여 문장을 완성하시오.

보기
그는 불을 켜놓은 채 자고 있었다. (with, turn, on, light)
→ He was sleeping with the light turned on.

그 소녀는 칠판에 눈을 고정시킨 채 수업을 듣고 있었다.
(with, fix, on the board, her eyes)
→ The girl was listening to the lecture ________
________.

고난도

25 서술형 심화

그림을 보고 〈보기〉에서 의미상 알맞은 문장을 골라 (1)~(3)에 분사구문이 들어간 문장을 완성하시오.

(1)

(2)

(3)

보기
ⓐ He waved his hand to his friends.
ⓑ I got first prize in the contest.
ⓒ She was holding her baby in her arms.

(1) ________, I was so proud of myself.

(2) Terry got on the train, ________.

(3) ________, Tiffany looked very happy.

CHAPTER 05

수동태

수동태

주어와 동사가 어떤 관계인지 나타내는 형식을 태(voice)라고 하고, 능동태와 수동태, 두 가지가 있다. 주어가 동작을 스스로 행하는 경우에는 **능동태**로 표현하고, 주어가 행동을 받거나 당하는 상황이면 **수동태**로 표현한다. 수동태는 기본적으로 「be동사 + 과거분사(p.p.)」로 쓰고, 형식과 시제에 따라 조금씩 달리 표현한다.

한눈에 쏙! 문법 Chart

• 수동태를 쓰는 경우

1. 동작을 행한 주체가 누구인지 불분명하거나 굳이 밝힐 필요가 없을 때
   - My cell phone **was stolen** yesterday. (누가 훔쳐갔는지 모름)
   - Rome **was not built** in a day (by people). (by people이 생략됨)
2. 동작을 행한 주체보다 동작을 받는 대상을 더 강조하고 싶을 때
   - My cell phone **was found** in a waste basket. (누가 발견했느냐 보다는, 핸드폰이 발견된 것을 강조)

• 수동태의 형태

수동태 문장의 기본 형태	주어 + be동사 + 과거분사(p.p.) + (by + 행위자) David **is loved** by everybody.
조동사가 있는 경우	주어 + 조동사 + be동사 + 과거분사(p.p.) + (by + 행위자) The problem **can be solved** (by us).
진행형	주어 + be동사 + being + 과거분사(p.p.) + (by + 행위자) The birthday cake **is being baked** by my mom.
완료형	주어 + have[has, had] been + 과거분사(p.p.) + (by + 행위자) His cellphone **has been found** (by him) in the library.
목적어로 쓰인 that절의 수동태	It + be동사 + 과거분사(p.p.) + that절 ~. **It is said that** honesty is the best policy. (= Honesty **is said to be** the best policy.)

핵심만 쏙! 문법 Point

Point 01 행위자에 초점을 두면 능동태, 행위의 대상에 초점을 두면 수동태를 써요!

- 수동태 문장의 기본 형태: 「주어 + be동사 + 과거분사(p.p.) + (by + 행위자)」의 형태로 나타낸다.

Many people around the world admire him. 전 세계의 많은 사람들이 그를 존경한다. (능동태)

He is admired by many people around the world. 그는 전 세계의 많은 사람들에 의해 존경 받는다. (수동태)

Point 02 수동태의 부정문은 「주어 + be동사 + not + 과거분사(p.p.)」로, 의문문은 「의문사 + be동사 + 주어 + 과거분사~?」의 형태로 나타내요!

The window was not broken by us. 그 창문은 우리에 의해 깨지지 않았다.

How much money is needed to pay it off? 그것을 지불하기 위해서는 얼마가 필요한가요?

> ※ 목적어를 갖지 않는 자동사(appear, disappear, happen, occur, become 등), 소유를 나타내는 동사(have, belong to), 상태를 나타내는 동사(resemble) 등은 수동태로 나타낼 수 없다.
>
> The man was disappeared all of a sudden. (X) → The man disappeared all of a sudden.

Point 03 조동사가 포함된 문장의 수동태는 「조동사 + be + 과거분사(p.p.)」의 형태로 써요!

We will keep the secret forever. 우리는 평생 그 비밀을 지킬 것이다.

The secret will be kept by us forever. 그 비밀은 우리에 의해 평생 지켜질 것이다.

Point 04 구동사가 있는 능동태 문장을 수동태로 전환할 경우, 구동사를 한 덩어리로 취급해요!

- 자주 쓰는 구동사 표현의 수동태: 구동사가 있는 능동태 문장을 수동태로 전환할 때는 이 구동사를 한 덩어리로 취급한다. 즉, 동사는 「be동사 + p.p.」로 바꾸고 전치사나 부사는 그대로 쓴다.

bring up (~를 기르다) → be brought up	look after (~을 돌보다) → be looked after
call off (~을 취소하다) → be called off	look down on (~를 돌보다) → be taken care of
carry out (~을 수행하다) → be carried out	make fun of (~을 놀리다) → be made fun of
deal with (~을 다루다) → be dealt with	pay for (~을 지불하다) → be paid for
give up (~을 포기하다) → be given up	put off (~를 연기하다) → be put off
hand in (~을 제출하다) → be handed in	put on (~을 입다) → be put on
laugh at (~을 비웃다) → be laughed at	turn on/off (~을 켜다/끄다) → be turned on/off

Mr. Kim's team will carry out the survey. Mr. Kim의 팀이 그 설문 조사를 수행할 것이다.

→ The survey will be carried out by Mr. Kim's team.

그 설문조사는 Mr. Kim의 팀에 의해 수행될 것이다.

His grandparents brought up John. 그의 조부모님께서 John을 기르셨다.

→ John was brought up by his grandparents. John은 그의 조부모님에 의해 길러졌다.

핵심만 콕! 문법 Check

A

괄호 안에서 알맞은 말을 고르시오.

1 His new movie was (released, releasing) yesterday.

2 People say Jenny (resembles, is resembled) her father.

3 Do you know what (happened, was happened) here?

4 Who is going to (prepare, be prepared) for the event?

B

다음을 수동태 문장으로 바꿀 때, 빈칸에 알맞은 말을 쓰시오.

1 People criticized him for his bad manners.

→ He ________ ________ for his bad manners.

2 The bad weather delayed the flight.

→ The flight ________ ________ by the bad weather.

3 A famous artist painted his portrait.

→ His portrait ________ ________ by a famous artist.

C

우리말과 뜻이 같도록 괄호 안의 말을 바르게 배열하여 문장을 완성하시오.

1 그 어려운 문제는 그에 의해 해결될 수 있다. (can, solve)

→ The difficult question ________ ________ ________ by him.

2 오늘 밤에 어떤 영화가 상영되나요? (will, show)

→ What movie ________ ________ ________ tonight?

3 그 책들은 다음 주까지 반납되어야 한다. (must, return)

→ The books ________ ________ ________ by next week.

D

밑줄 친 부분에 유의하여 각 문장을 수동태로 바꿔 쓰시오.

1 The teacher <u>called off</u> the school trip.

→ ____.

2 They <u>take care of</u> their baby.

→ ____.

3 Many people in his country <u>look up to</u> him.

→ ____.

핵심만 쏙! 문법 Point

Point 05 수동태의 진행형은 「be being p.p.」, 부정문은 「be not being + p.p.」!

Mom **is preparing** the food in the kitchen. 어머니께서는 부엌에서 음식을 준비하고 계신다.
→ The food is being prepared by mom in the kitchen. 음식은 부엌에서 어머니에 의해 준비 되고 있다.
They **are not cleaning** the room now. 그들은 지금 방을 치우고 있지 않다.
→ The room is not being cleaned by them now. 그 방은 그들에 의해 치워지지 않고 있다.

Point 06 수동태의 완료형은 「have been p.p.」, 부정문은 「have not been p.p.」!

I **have completed** the report perfectly. 나는 보고서를 완벽하게 마무리했다.
→ The report has been completed perfectly by me.
→ The report has not been completed perfectly by me.

Point 07 4형식 문장에서는 능동태 문장에서의 직접목적어와 간접목적어를 각각 주어로 하여 두 가지 수동태를 만들 수 있어요!

능동태(4형식 문장)	Sally gave me(간·목) some souvenirs(직·목) from her trip to New York.
직접목적어가 주어인 수동태	Some souvenirs were given **to me** by Sally from her trip to New York.
간접목적어가 주어인 수동태	I was given **some souvenirs** by Sally from her trip to New York.

※ 단, 직접목적어를 주어로 하는 수동태의 경우, 4형식 문장을 3형식 문장으로 바꿀 때처럼, 간접목적어 앞에 to, for, of 중에서 적절한 전치사를 써야 한다.

to를 쓰는 동사	teach, give, sell, send, show, tell, bring
for를 쓰는 동사	make, buy, cook, get, build
of를 쓰는 동사	ask, inquire

Mr. Park taught us English.
→ We were taught English by Mr. Park.
→ English was taught to us my Mr. Park.

- 다음 동사들은 **직접목적어만 수동태의 주어로** 쓸 수 있다.

make, buy, cook, get, write, pass, sell, find 등

Mom **cooked** me delicious soup. 엄마는 내게 맛있는 수프를 만들어 주셨다.
→ Delicious soup was cooked for me by mom. (O)
→ I was cooked delicious soup by mom. (X)

Point 08 5형식의 수동태에서 목적격보어는 「be p.p.」 뒤에 그대로 이어서 써요!

- 5형식 문장을 수동태로 전환할 때는 목적어만 수동태의 주어가 될 수 있다.

We **called** the puppy Coco. 우리는 강아지를 Coco라고 불렀다.
→ The puppy **was called** Coco by us. 그 강아지는 우리에 의해 Coco라고 불렸다.
→ Coco was called the puppy by us. (X) (→ 목적격 보어는 수동태의 주어로 쓸 수 없다.)

핵심만 콕! 문법 Check

A 괄호 안에서 알맞은 말을 고르시오.

1 The trees (are cutting, are being cut) now.
2 The car (is not being, is being not) fixed by dad.
3 The room had already (cleaned, been cleaned) by us.
4 The event has (being, been) prepared by all the students.

B 능동태는 수동태로, 수동태는 능동태 문장으로 바꿔 쓸 때 빈칸에 알맞은 말을 쓰시오.

1 Jane has organized the files in the drawer.
→ The files in the drawer ______ ______ ______ by Jane.

2 Mr. White has taught us English for two years.
→ English ______ ______ ______ to us by Mr. White for two years.

C 우리말과 뜻이 같도록 괄호 안의 말을 바르게 배열하여 문장을 완성하시오.

1 Peter는 엄마에게 약간의 용돈을 받았다. (given, was, his mom, by, allowances, some)
→ Peter ______________________________.

2 약간의 용돈이 엄마에 의해 Peter에게 주어졌다. (were, by, his mom, given, to, Peter)
→ Some allowances ______________________________.

D 5형식 문장을 수동태로 바꾼 문장에서, 어법상 틀린 부분을 찾아 바르게 고쳐 쓰시오.

1 He asked me to come with Jane.
→ I was asked come with Jane by him. ______ → ______

2 They named their cat Nabi.
→ Their cat was named to Nabi by them. ______ → ______

3 The doctor asked me to start exercising.
→ I was asked to starting exercising by the doctor. ______ → ______

4 My mother told me to buy some groceries.
→ I was told buying some groceries by my mother. ______ → ______

핵심만 쏙! 문법 Point

Point 09 5형식 문장에서 목적격보어로 쓰인 동사원형은 수동태로 바꿀 때 to부정사로 바꿔요!

(1) 5형식 문장을 수동태로 바꿀 때 목적격보어로 쓰인 동사원형(원형부정사)은 to부정사로 바꾼다.

I heard someone call my name. 나는 누군가가 내 이름을 부르는 것을 들었다.

→ Someone was heard to call my name. 누군가 내 이름을 부르는 것이 들려졌다.

Mom made me turn off the TV. 엄마는 내게 TV를 끄게 시켰다.

→ I was made to turn off the TV by Mom. 나는 엄마에 의해 TV를 끄도록 시켜졌다.

(2) 5형식 문장을 수동태로 바꿀 때 목적격보어로 쓰인 분사는 「be p.p.」뒤에 그대로 이어서 쓴다.

I heard someone calling my name.

→ Someone was heard calling my name.

Point 10 사역동사 let과 have의 수동태는 「be let」,「be had」가 아니에요!

- 사역동사 let은 「be allowed to + 동사원형」, have는 「be asked to + 동사원형」의 형태로 수동태를 만든다.

Our teacher let us play outside. 우리 선생님께서 우리가 밖에서 노는 것을 허락하셨다.

→ We were allowed by our teacher to play outside.

I had my brother clean his room. 나는 남동생에게 그의 방을 치우도록 했다.

→ My brother was asked to clean his room.

Point 11 목적어가 that절인 경우는 두 가지 방법으로 수동태 전환이 가능해요!

- 동사 believe, consider, expect, know, say, suppose, think등과 같은 동사가 목적어로 that절을 취할 경우:

(1) 「가주어(It) + be동사 + 과거분사(p.p.) + that절」로 바꿀 수 있다.

(2) 「that절의 주어 + be동사 + 과거분사(p.p.) + to동사원형(that절 내의 동사)」로 바꿀 수 있다.

They say that Mr. White is a very reliable person.
그들은 Mr. White이 매우 믿을만한 사람이라고 말한다.

→ [That Mr. White is a very reliable person] is said (by them).

→ (1) It is said [that Mr. White is a very reliable person]. (가주어 it, 진주어 that절)

→ (2) Mr. White is said to be a very reliable person. (주어 Mr. White, 동사구는 to부정사)

Point 12 by이외의 전치사를 쓰는 수동태들이 있어요!

be ashamed of	~을 부끄러워하다	be known for	~로 유명하다
be based on	~에 근거를 두다	be known to	~에게 알려지다
be bored with	~에 지겨워지다	be made from	~로 만들어지다 (재료의 성질 변화)
be covered with	~으로 덮여 있다	be made of	~로 만들어지다 (재료의 모양 변화)
be composed of	~으로 구성되다	be pleased with	~에 기쁘다
be crowded with	~으로 혼잡하다	be satisfied with	~에 만족하다
be disappointed with	~에 실망하다	be shocked at	~에 충격을 받다
be filled with	~으로 가득 차다	be surprised by(at)	~에 놀라다
be interested in	~에 관심이 있다	be tired of	~에 싫증나다
be known as	~로서 알려지다	be worried about	~에 대해 걱정하다

This table was made of wood. 이 탁자는 나무로 만들어졌다.

The cheese was made from the best quality milk. 그 치즈는 최상급 품질의 우유로 만들어졌다.

핵심만 콕! 문법 Check

A 괄호 안에서 알맞은 말을 고르시오.

1 Birds were heard (sing, to sing) in the forest.

2 We were made (helping, to help) him wash his car.

3 I was (allowed, let) to borrow some of her clothes.

B 우리말과 뜻이 같도록 괄호 안의 말을 활용하여 문장을 완성하시오.

1 야구를 하는 아이들이 창문을 깨는 것이 우리에 의해 목격되었다. (see, break)

→ Children playing baseball ________ ________ ________ ________ the window by us.

2 우리는 엄마에 의해 집안일을 하게 되었다. (made, do)

→ We ________ ________ ________ ________ housework by our mom.

C 다음을 〈보기〉와 같이 두 개의 수동태 문장으로 바꿔 쓰시오.

보기

People believed that what he said was true.
→ It was believed that what he said was true.
→ What he said was believed to be true.

1 People suppose that his movie is great.

→ ____

→ ____

2 People say that eating an apple a day keeps the doctor away.

→ ____

→ ____

D 우리말과 뜻이 같도록 괄호 안의 말을 활용하여 빈칸에 알맞은 말을 쓰시오.

1 그는 회사의 모든 사람들에게 알려져 있다. (know)

→ He is ________________ ________________ everyone in the office.

2 그 영화는 실제 이야기에 근거를 두고 있다. (base)

→ The movie is ________________ ________________ a real-life story.

내신 만점! 실전 기출

[1~2] 다음을 수동태 문장으로 바꿀 때, 빈칸에 알맞은 것을 고르시오.

01

You must keep the milk in the refrigerator.
→ The milk __________ in the refrigerator.

① must kept be ② must being kept
③ must be kept ④ must be keeping
⑤ must have kept

02

He has composed many great songs for years.
→ Many great songs __________ by him for years.

① are composing ② were composing
③ were composed ④ have been composed
⑤ have being composed

[3~4] 빈칸에 공통으로 알맞은 말을 고르시오.

03

- We were all bored ⓐ __________ the endless speech made by the principal.
- My heart was filled ⓑ __________ joy when I heard the news.

① with ② at ③ of
④ on ⑤ as

04

- Some of the rules are ⓐ __________ written on the board.
- The room was ⓑ __________ painted by two people.

① have ② being ③ been
④ having been ⑤ having being

05 서술형

어법에 맞지 않는 부분을 찾아 바르게 고쳐 쓰시오.

For safety, passwords should change every six months.
(안전을 위해 비밀번호는 6개월마다 변경되어야만 한다.)

__________ → __________

06 빈칸에 알맞은 말이 나머지 넷과 다른 하나는?

① A secret tip was given __________ them.
② Some papers were passed __________ us.
③ The e-mail was sent __________ me yesterday.
④ Some items were sold __________ us by them.
⑤ A new suitcase was bought __________ me by dad.

07 다음을 수동태 문장으로 바꿀 때 빈칸 ⓐ~ⓑ에 알맞은 말이 순서대로 나열된 것은?

- The coach made him stop playing after the injury.
  → He was made ⓐ __________ playing by coach after the injury.
- My sister let me use her laptop computer.
  → I ⓑ __________ her laptop computer by my sister.

① stop, was let use
② stopping, was allowed to use
③ to stop, was allowed to use
④ stopped, was let use
⑤ having stopped, was allowed using

08 다음을 수동태 문장으로 바꿀 때 빈칸에 알맞은 말은?

> The interviewer asked me many difficult questions.
> → Many difficult questions were asked ________ me by the interviewer.

① for ② of ③ to
④ with ⑤ from

09 밑줄 친 부분이 어법상 틀린 것은?

① I was bored with my routine life.
② We are not interested in history.
③ The man was ashamed of his mistake.
④ Sally was known for her nice personality.
⑤ The tourist was amazed to the beautiful scenery.

10 다음을 수동태 문장으로 바꿀 때 빈칸에 알맞은 말은?

> It is believed that Koreans are hardworking and diligent.
> → Koreans ________ hardworking and diligent.

① believe be ② believe being
③ believe to be ④ are believed to be
⑤ are believed being

[11~12] 다음을 주어진 단어로 시작하는 수동태 문장으로 고쳐 쓰시오.

11 서술형

> Everyone in his class called Jack captain.

→ Jack ______________________________
______________________________.

12 서술형

> His teacher offered him a great opportunity.

→ (1) He ______________________________
______________________________.

→ (2) A great opportunity ______________________________
______________________________.

13 능동태 문장을 수동태 문장으로 바꾼 것 중 잘못된 것은?

① They have canceled the appointment.
→ The appointment has been canceled by them.
② He asked me to go to the movies with him.
→ I was asked to go to the movies with him.
③ My father bought me these glasses.
→ These glasses were bought for me by my father.
④ They elected him president last week.
→ President was elected by him last week.
⑤ The doctor must treat the patient with the medication.
→ The patient must be treated with the medication by the doctor.

최다빈출

14 빈칸에 알맞은 말이 나머지와 다른 하나는?

① We were pleased ________ the result.
② His face was filled ________ happiness.
③ He looks satisfied ________ his job.
④ They must be disappointed ________ my behavior.
⑤ We are tired ________ the same dish every day.

15 밑줄 친 문장을 주어로 하는 수동태 문장을 만들 수 없는 것은?

① He showed me the old book.
② We heard him play the violin.
③ Everyone thinks him a genius.
④ He taught me how to solve the equation.
⑤ Her beautiful smile makes everyone happy.

16 서술형

다음을 주어진 단어로 시작하는 수동태 문장으로 바꿔 쓰시오.

People say that Ji-sung Park is one of the best soccer players.

→ (1) Ji-sung Park ______________________
______________________.

→ (2) It ______________________
______________________.

17 밑줄 친 전치사의 쓰임이 올바른 것은?

① A new bag was bought to me by her.
② A question was asked of Jane by a new student.
③ A love letter was given for her by John.
④ A scholarship was offered of him by the university.
⑤ Some delicious cookies are baked to kids by my mom.

18 밑줄 친 부분의 쓰임이 잘못된 것을 모두 고르면?

① We were all surprised at the scene.
② His name is well-known as many people.
③ The desk was covered of a lot of documents.
④ The inside was filled with plants and trees.
⑤ All of them were worried about their exam results.

신유형

19 서술형

주어진 조건에 맞춰 다음을 영작할 때 5번째로 올 단어를 쓰시오.

조건

1. 'the books'를 주어로 문장 맨 처음에 쓰시오.
2. 총 10개의 단어로 이루어진 완전한 영어 문장을 쓰시오.
3. 'possible'이라는 단어를 포함하시오.

그 책들은 가능한 빨리 반납되는 편이 좋겠다.

→ ______________________
____

20 어법상 틀린 문장을 모두 고르면?

ⓐ Is the food being made by her?
ⓑ My hair was cut too short.
ⓒ He was elected by chairman by them.
ⓓ They were heard arguing about something.
ⓔ The boys were made being quiet by their mom.

① ⓐ, ⓑ ② ⓑ, ⓒ ③ ⓒ, ⓓ
④ ⓒ, ⓔ ⑤ ⓒ, ⓓ, ⓔ

21 수동태로 전환한 문장이 어법상 틀린 것은?

① He is repairing his bicycle now.
→ His bicycle is being repaired by him now.
② My mother runs a small bakery.
→ A small bakery is run by my mother.
③ People think he works very hard.
→ He is thought to work very hard.
④ We can recycle most waste these days.
→ Most waste can be recycled these days.
⑤ Tiffany will teach us English next year.
→ We will be taught to English by Tiffany next year.

22 밑줄 친 부분이 어법상 틀린 것은?

A: Hey, did you hear the news?
B: What news?
A: It's not good news actually. A fire ⓐ was broken out at the shopping mall near our neighborhood.
B: Really? ⓑ Was anyone killed?
A: No one ⓒ was reported to die. According to the radio news, firefighters are ⓓ trying to put out the fire, but smoke still ⓔ can be seen.

① ⓐ ② ⓑ ③ ⓒ
④ ⓓ ⑤ ⓔ

신유형

23 서술형

우리말과 뜻이 같도록 〈보기〉에서 알맞은 단어를 골라 문장을 완성하시오. (단, 필요한 단어만 골라 사용하시오.)

조건

is	looked	look	up
down	to	on	by
looking	people	much	many

이순신은 많은 사람들에 의해 존경을 받는다.

→ Commander Lee Sun-shin ______________
______________________________.

고난도

24 다음 ⓐ~ⓒ에 알맞은 말이 순서대로 바르게 짝지어진 것은?

What is the greatest invention of all time? Many people would answer that it is the computer. A computer is a device that can be ⓐ __________ to carry out a set of logical operations automatically. Since a sequence of operations can be varied, the computer can ⓑ __________ more than one kind of problem. So, who invented the computer? It is known that Charles Babbage, an English mechanical engineer, originated the concept of the computer. He is ⓒ __________ "the father of the computer."

	ⓐ		ⓑ		ⓒ
①	programming	—	solved	—	considering
②	programmed	—	solving	—	considering
③	programmed	—	solved	—	considered
④	programming	—	solve	—	considered
⑤	programmed	—	solve	—	considered

고난도

25 서술형 심화

다음은 미나네 학급 규칙이다. 밑줄 친 부분이 어법상 틀린 부분을 두 군데 찾아 바르게 고쳐 쓰시오.

< Class Rules >
(1) Food should not be ate during class.
(2) Homework should be done before class.
(3) Only English must be spoken in the class.
(4) Cell phones must be turn off during class.

______________ → ______________
______________ → ______________

CHAPTER 06

접속사

접속사

접속사는 단어와 단어, 구와 구, 또는 절과 절을 **연결해 주는 말**이다. 하는 역할에 따라 **등위접속사**와 **종속접속사**로 구분할 수 있다.

- **접속사의 쓰임**

접속사	단어와 단어를 연결	Sally ate bread **and** cheese.
	구와 구를 연결	Hurry up **and** open the door.
	절과 절을 연결	**When** I visited Sam, he was just about to bake some cookies.
		We know **that** he is honest and trustworthy.

- 구(phrase): '주어 + 동사'를 포함하지 않으면서 둘 이상의 단어가 모여 하나의 품사 역할을 하는 것
- 절(clause): '주어 + 동사'를 포함하고 있으며 둘 이상의 단어가 모여 문장의 일부를 이루는 것

한눈에 쏙! 문법 Chart

종속접속사	부사절을 이끌 때	시간	when(~할 때), while(~하는 동안), as(~하고 있을 때, ~하면서), before(~하기 전에), after(~후에), since(~이래로), until(~할 때까지)
		이유	because, since, as(~이니까, ~때문에)
		조건	if(만일 ~한다면), unless(만일 ~하지 않는다면)
		양보	though, even though, although(비록 ~이지만, ~임에도 불구하고)
		대조	while(~하는 반면에)
	명사절을 이끌 때	that	(1) 주어, 목적어, 보어 역할. (2) 목적어절을 이끌 때의 접속사 that은 생략할 수 있다.
		if, whether	(1) '~인지 아닌지'. 주어, 목적어, 보어 역할 (2) if는 문장의 주어로 쓰이는 명사절을 이끌지 못한다.
	결과를 나타낼 때		「so + 형용사/부사 + that + 주어 + can ~」(너무 ~해서 …한) = 「형용사/부사 + enough to + 동사원형」(…하기에 충분히 ~한) 「so + 형용사/부사 + that + 주어 + can't ~」(…하기엔 너무 ~한) = 「too + 형용사/부사 + to + 동사원형」(너무 ~해서 …할 수 없는)
	목적을 나타낼 때		「so that + 주어 + 동사」(~하기 위해, ~하도록) = 「in order to + 동사원형」 = 「so as to + 동사원형」
상관접속사	복수취급		both A and B (A와 B 둘 다)
	B가 주어		not A but B (A가 아닌 B) either A or B (A나 B 둘 중 하나) neither A nor B (A도 B도 아닌) not only A but also B = B as well as A (A뿐만 아니라 B도)
접속부사	대조		however(그러나), on the other hand(반면에)
	결과		therefore(그러므로), as a result(결과적으로)
	첨가		in addition(덧붙여, 게다가), besides(게다가), moreover(게다가)
	예시		for example(예를 들면), for instance(예를 들면)

핵심만 쏙! 문법 Point

Point 01 종속접속사는 종속절을 주절에 연결해주는 접속사예요!

- 시간: **when**(~할 때), **while**(~하는 동안), **as**(~하고 있을 때, ~하면서), **before**(~전에), **after**(~후에), **since**(~이래로), **until**(~할 때까지)
  When I arrived at school, the gate was closed. 내가 학교에 도착했을 때, 문이 닫혀있었다.
  I listened to music while I was doing my homework. 나는 숙제를 하는 동안 음악을 들었다.
- 이유: **because**, **since**, **as**(~이니까, ~때문에)

  ※ 이유의 강도: because(~하기 때문에) > since (~하니까) > as (~하므로)

  I need to hurry up because I'm late for class. 나는 수업에 늦었기 때문에 서둘러야 해.
  As you are here, let's move the furniture together. 네가 여기 있으니 한께 가구를 옮기자.
  ※ because 뒤에는 '주어 + 동사', because of 뒤에는 '명사(구)'가 온다.
- 조건: **if**(만일 ~한다면), **unless**(만일 ~하지 않는다면)
  If it is nice this afternoon, I will go to the park. 만일 오후에 날씨가 좋으면, 나는 공원에 갈 것이다.
  Unless it rains hard, I will walk to school. = If it does not rain hard, I will walk to school.
- 양보: **though**, **even though**, **although**(비록 ~이지만, ~임에도 불구하고)
  Although he is poor, he is not sad. 그는 가난함에도 불구하고 슬프지 않다.
- 대조: **while**(~하는 반면에)
  He likes Italian food, while she likes Korean food.
- 결과:
  (1) 「**so + 형용사/부사 + that + 주어 + can ~**」(너무 ~해서 …한) = 「**형용사/부사 + enough to + 동사원형**」(…하기에 충분히 ~한)
  Eric is so strong that he can carry the box. = Eric is strong enough to carry the box.
  (2) 「**so + 형용사/부사 + that + 주어 + can't ~**」(…하기엔 너무 ~한) = 「**too + 형용사/부사 + to + 동사원형**」(너무 ~해서 …할 수 없는)
  I am so nervous that I can't make a presentation.
  = I am too nervous to make a presentation.
- 목적: 「**so that ~**」:「**so that + 주어 + 동사**」(~하기 위해, ~하도록) = 「**in order to + 동사원형**」 = 「**so as to + 동사원형**」
  I save money so that I can buy a new car. = I save money in order to buy a new car.
- **명사절을 이끄는 that**: 「접속사 + 주어 + 동사」로 주어, 목적어(생략 가능), 보어 역할
  (1) 주어: That he is smart is obvious. 그가 똑똑하다는 것은 확실하다.
  (2) 목적어: I believe (that) it will be a White Christmas. 나는 화이트 크리스마스가 될 것을 믿는다.
  (3) 보어: The important thing is that we have to finish it. 중요한 것은 우리가 그것을 끝내야 한다는 것이다.
- **명사절을 이끄는 if나 whether**: 「if[whether] + 주어 + 동사」(~인지 아닌지), 보어 역할

주어	Whether she will meet him or not is uncertain. 그녀가 그를 만날지 안 만날지는 확실하지 않다. ※ 주어로 온 명사절에는 whether만 쓴다. if는 주어절을 이끌 수 없다.
목적어	Let's ask her if[whether] she can make it for us. 그녀가 우리를 위해 그 일을 해줄 수 있나 물어보자. ※ 〈to부정사 앞〉이나 〈전치사 뒤〉에는 whether를 쓰고, if는 쓸 수 없다. I can't decide whether to take the test or not. 그 시험을 치를지 어떨지 결정 못하겠다.
보어	The problem is if[whether] they can come on time. 문제는 그들이 제시간에 올 수 있을지 여부이다.

- 간접의문문 형태
  (1) 의문사가 있는 경우: 「의문사 + 주어+ 동사」
  I don't know. + **What time is it** now? → I don't know what time it is now.
  (2) 의문사가 없는 경우: 「**if[whether]** + 주어 + 동사」'~인지 아닌지'
  I wonder. + Will the movie be interesting? → I wonder if[whether] the movie will be interesting.

핵심만 콕! 문법 Check

A 괄호 안에서 알맞은 말을 고르시오.

1 The pants are too big for me (that, to) wear.
2 It was so delicious (that, to) everyone liked it.
3 (That, Whether) he is rich or not is not important.
4 (Since, After) the weather is fine, we will go on a picnic.
5 The article tells (if, that) we will have about a 2-week break.
6 (As, Until) the movie was fun, she bought the original novel.
7 Tim is very good at English, (after, while) his brother is absolutely not.

B 밑줄 친 부분에 유의하여 우리말로 해석하시오.

1 I don't know <u>if</u> my mom is at home.
→ ______________________________

2 He asked <u>when</u> the bus would arrive.
→ ______________________________

3 I watched Titanic three times <u>since</u> it was so fun and romantic.
→ ______________________________

4 <u>Even though</u> he is only 4 years old, he can write his name neatly.
→ ______________________________

C 두 문장의 뜻이 같도록 빈칸에 알맞은 말을 쓰시오.

1 His voice is so soft that I cannot understand it.
→ His voice is too ______________________________ understand.

2 People study English hard so that they can communicate with people around the world.
→ People study English hard in ______________________________ around the world.

D 두 문장을 한 문장으로 바꿔 쓰시오.

1 I wonder. + When is the party? → I wonder ______________________________.

2 Nobody knew. + Were the people safe?
→ Nobody knew ______________________________.

E 우리말과 같은 뜻이 되도록 괄호 안의 말을 활용하여 문장을 완성하시오.

1 문제는 그 소문이 사실이라는 것이다. (the rumor, true, is, that)
→ The problem is ______________________________.

2 그 공이 너무 빨라서 나는 칠 수가 없었다. (so, that, fast, I, couldn't)
→ The ball was ______________________________ hit it.

3 우체국이 어디에 있는지 말씀해 주실래요? (tell, is, me, where, the post office)
→ Can you ______________________________?

핵심만 쏙! 문법 Point

Point 02 상관접속사는 문법적으로 대등한 품사를 연결해요!

- 자주 쓰이는 상관접속사 표현

상관접속사 종류	의미	주어로 올 때 동사의 수 일치
both *A* and *B*	*A*와 *B* 둘 다	동사의 복수형을 취함
not *A* but *B*	*A*가 아닌 *B*	동사의 수는 B에 일치
either *A* or *B*	*A*나 *B* 둘 중 하나	
neither *A* nor *B*	*A*도 *B*도 아닌	
not only *A* but also *B*	*A*뿐만 아니라 *B*도	
B as well as *A*		

Both **Tim** and **Jack** **like** playing soccer. Tim과 Jack은 둘 다 축구 하는 것을 좋아한다.
It is not I but he that **knows** the answer. 답을 아는 것은 내가 아니라 그이다.
Either Nick or you **have** to go there. Nick이나 너 둘 중 하나는 거기에 가야 한다.
Neither Sarah nor **I am** not responsible for that. Sarah도 나도 그것에 책임이 있지 않다.
Not only the children but also their mother **likes** to watch the TV program.
= Their mother as well as the children **likes** to watch the TV program.
아이들뿐만 아니라 그들의 엄마도 그 TV프로그램 보는 것을 좋아한다.

Point 03 「명령문 + and …」(~해라, 그러면 …할 것이다), 「명령문 + or …」(~해라, 그렇지 않으면 …할 것이다) 라는 뜻이에요!

- 「명령문 + and …」 = 「If you + 동사의 현재형, you + (조)동사 ~」(~해라, 그러면 …할 것이다)

Practice hard, and you'll win the game. 열심히 연습해라, 그러면 경기에서 이길 것이다.
→ If you practice hard, you'll win the game.

- 「명령문 + or …」 = 「If you don't + 동사원형, you + (조)동사 ~」 = 「Unless you + 동사의 현재형, you + (조)동사 ~」(~해라, 그렇지 않으면 …할 것이다)

Hurry up, or you'll be late for school. 서둘러라. 그렇지 않으면, 너는 학교에 늦을 것이다.
→ If you don't hurry up, you'll be late for school.
→ Unless you hurry up, you'll be late for school.

Point 04 접속부사는 접속사의 뜻을 나타내는 부사로서 절과 절을 연결할 수 없고, 문장에서의 위치가 자유롭고 단독으로도 쓰일 수 있어요!

- 자주 쓰이는 상관접속사 표현

ⓐ 대조	however (그러나), on the other hand (반면에)
ⓑ 결과	therefore (그러므로), as a result (결과적으로)
ⓒ 첨가	in addition (덧붙여, 게다가), besides (게다가), moreover (게다가)
ⓓ 예시	for example (예를 들면), for instance (예를 들면)

ⓐ It was hot. However, I drank hot tea. 날이 더웠다. 그러나 나는 뜨거운 차를 마셨다.
ⓑ It was hot. Therefore, I ate some ice cream. 날이 더웠다. 그래서 나는 아이스크림을 먹었다.
ⓒ It was hot. In addition, the air conditioner was broken. 날이 더웠다. 게다가, 에어컨이 고장 났다.
ⓓ It was hot. Cold drinks, for example, iced water and soft drinks, helped me to cool down.
날이 더웠다. 차가운 음료, 예를 들어 얼음 물, 탄산음료가 나의 더위를 식히는데 도움을 주었다.

핵심만 콕! 문법 Check

A

괄호 안에서 알맞은 말을 고르시오.

1 Neither Jason (or, nor) Becky will pass the exam.
2 Both Mr. Jackson (or, and) Mrs. Jackson like Italian food.
3 Not Ben (and, but) Sarah wants to have a surprise party.
4 Either my mom (or, nor) my dad is going to pick me up.
5 I enjoy watching not only horror movies (but, and) also comedy movies.

B

접속사를 활용하여 〈보기〉와 같이 바꿔 쓸 때 빈칸에 알맞은 말을 쓰시오.

보기

ⓐ Go to the zoo, and your son will love it.
→ If you go to the zoo, your son will love it.

ⓑ Obey the rule, or you have to pay the fine.
→ If you don't obey the rule, you have to pay the fine.
→ Unless you obey the rule, you have to pay the fine.

1 Take public transportation, and you will save time.
→ ______________________, you will save time.

2 Run, or you'll be late for the lesson.
→ ______________________, you'll be late for the lesson.
→ ______________________, you'll be late for the lesson.

C

빈칸에 알맞은 말을 〈보기〉에서 골라 쓰시오.

보기

Therefore　　　However　　　Moreover

1 The day was cold. ______________________, it was raining.
2 That is mine. ______________________, you may use it if you want to.
3 He had a high fever. ______________________, he took some medicine.

D

우리말과 뜻이 같도록 괄호 안의 말을 바르게 배열하여 문장을 완성하시오.

1 Tina는 소고기도 돼지고기도 좋아하지 않는다. (beef, neither, pork, nor)
→ Tina likes ______________________.

2 그녀는 예쁘다. 게다가 똑똑하다. (in, she, addition, smart, is,)
→ She is pretty. ______________________.

3 조용히 해라, 그렇지 않으면 잠자는 아기가 깰 것이다. (sleeping, or, wake, baby, the, will, up)
→ Be quiet, ______________________.

4 그녀는 변호사나 경찰 둘 중 하나가 되고 싶어한다. (a lawyer, or, a police officer, either)
→ She wants to be ______________________.

5 열심히 공부해라, 그러면 너의 꿈은 현실이 될 것이다. (true, and, will, come, your dreams)
→ Study hard, ______________________.

내신 만점! 실전 기출

01 밑줄 친 while의 의미가 나머지와 다른 하나는?

① Please take care of my puppy while I'm away.
② My sister is very good at English, while I'm not.
③ I usually listen to music while I clean the house.
④ He usually eats potato chips while he is watching TV.
⑤ It's not safe to talk on the phone while you're driving a car.

02 어법상 틀린 문장은?

① I wonder that Ann needs my help.
② He'll definitely help you if you want.
③ Do you know if they came to class on time?
④ Julie asked me whether I could come to her house.
⑤ I am very curious if there are other living things out there.

03 〈보기〉의 밑줄 친 while과 의미하는 바가 같은 것은?

> 보기
> While we were hiking, we enjoyed beautiful mountain scenery.

① She is taking a break for a while.
② While Sue likes English, Tom likes science.
③ Please don't listen to music while you are studying.
④ It took quite a while for him to recover from his sickness.
⑤ While he is really good at making things, his brother is hopeless.

04 빈칸에 공통으로 알맞은 접속사는?

> ⓐ Some people like juice, ________ others don't.
> ⓑ Turn off your electronic devices ________ you are flying on a plane.

① if ② after ③ while
④ since ⑤ until

05 어법상 어색한 것은?

① The table is so heavy that I can't move it.
② He was so tired that he could get up early.
③ The game was so exciting that I couldn't stop playing it.
④ She was so busy that she couldn't come on time.
⑤ The movie is so exciting that the tickets are all sold out.

06 서술형

빈칸에 공통으로 알맞은 접속사를 쓰시오.

> ⓐ ________ you know, Julia is the smartest girl in the class.
> ⓑ ________ science develops, robots will become a bigger part of our lives.

→ ____________________

최다빈출

07 밑줄 친 that의 쓰임이 나머지 넷과 다른 것은?

① I believe that he is innocent.
② She thinks that he is honest.
③ The truth is that it is just a rumor.
④ The problem is that I can't stop eating sweets.
⑤ I want to invent a machine that is useful for us.

08 〈보기〉와 의미하는 바가 같은 문장은?

보기
She is too sleepy to read the book.

① She is so sleepy that she reads the book.
② She is so sleepy that she can read the book.
③ She is so sleepy that she can't read the book.
④ She is so sleepy that she could read the book.
⑤ She is so sleepy that she couldn't read the book.

09 어법상 옳은 문장을 모두 고르면? (2개)

① I like not only you but also he.
② Jisu is not only pretty but also warm hearted.
③ Not only Eric but also I are going to attend the meeting.
④ They are learning not only speaking but also write in English.
⑤ Tim is good at not only playing soccer but also playing baseball.

10 〈보기〉의 as와 밑줄 친 부분의 쓰임이 같은 것은?

보기
We were able to see many stars in the sky as it got darker.

① The apple was as sweet as sugar.
② As she is new here, she may need some help.
③ The boy lost his umbrella as his mom said he would.
④ As she grew older, she became known to many people.
⑤ As you know, you'd better put a lot of effort into the project.

11 서술형

빈칸에 공통으로 알맞은 접속사를 쓰시오.

ⓐ He is so little ________ he can't stay home alone.
ⓑ She is so smart ________ she can answer the math questions easily.

→ ________________

12 밑줄 친 ⓐ if와 쓰임이 다른 하나는?

The boy wondered ⓐ if chickens could fly.

① Do you know if he has a girlfriend?
② Could you tell me if I am on the right track?
③ Mrs. Audrey asked me if I had turned in the paper.
④ My mom will get angry if I break my promise.
⑤ He wonders if he should buy a new cell phone.

13 서술형

우리말과 뜻이 같도록 괄호 안의 말을 활용하여 문장을 완성하시오.

학생들은 대개 새 학년이 시작되면 잘 할 지에 대해 걱정한다. (whether, do, well)

→ Students usually wonder ________________ ________ when a new school year begins.

14 〈보기〉의 문장과 같은 의미로 쓰인 것은?

보기
I concentrated on the lecture so hard that I could understand it well.

① I concentrated on the lecture in order to understand it well.
② I concentrated on the lecture too hard to understand it well.
③ I concentrated on the lecture hard enough to understand it well.
④ I concentrated on the lecture hard so that I could understand it well.
⑤ I concentrated on the lecture so hard that I couldn't understand it well.

15 서술형

두 문장의 뜻이 같도록 빈칸에 알맞은 말을 쓰시오.

He went to the library to return the books so that he would not pay the penalty.

= He went to the library to return the books in ________ ________ ________ pay the penalty.

16 〈보기〉에서 알맞은 말을 찾아 빈칸에 쓰시오. (필요 시 중복 사용 가능)

보기

until before since although unless

ⓐ The meeting lasted ________ 2:00.
ⓑ She waited for him at the bus stop ________ it rained heavily.
ⓒ The students must be in their seats ________ the teacher comes into the class.
ⓓ ________ you woke up late, you'd better hurry up in order not to miss the flight.

17 서술형

우리말과 뜻이 같도록 괄호 안의 말을 바르게 배열하여 문장을 완성하시오.

행복이 멀리 있는 것처럼 느껴질 수 있지만, 그것은 네가 생각하는 것보다 네게 더 가까이에 있을 수 있다.
(happiness, although, may, far, seem, away)

→ ________________
________________, it may be closer to you than you think.

18 빈칸에 알맞은 말이 순서대로 바르게 나열된 것은?

Kevin: What's your motto, Sarah?
Sarah: Well. 'Work hard, ________ you can't achieve anything.' How about you?
Kevin: 'Be an early bird, ________ you will get the worms.'
Sarah: Sounds great.

① and, or
② and, and
③ or, or
④ or, and
⑤ so, or

19 서술형

빈칸에 공통으로 알맞은 접속사 한 단어를 쓰시오.

ⓐ ________ it was freezing, he didn't wear socks.
ⓑ ________ the rumor turned out to be false, people still believed it.

→ ________________

20 서술형

우리말과 뜻이 같도록 영작하시오.

나는 선인장들이 밤에 산소를 내뿜을 뿐만 아니라 사람들의 숙면에 도움을 준다는 것을 알았다.

→ I knew that cactuses ________ ________ give out oxygen ________ ________ help people sleep well at night.

21 서술형

주어진 문장과 뜻이 같도록 괄호 안의 말을 활용하여 문장을 다시 쓰시오.

She stopped eating junk food in order to stay healthy.

→ ________________
________________ (so that)

22 빈칸에 알맞은 것은?

What am I? I have many different colors like red, yellow, and pink. People buy me on special days like on a birthday or Valentine's Day. Also, single men buy me and a ring to propose to their girlfriends. Some people use me not only to make tea ________ aromatherapy oil. Do you know what I am yet? I am a rose!

① to make ② but made
③ but also making ④ but also made
⑤ but also to make

23 서술형

괄호 안의 말을 활용하여 밑줄 친 부분을 영작하시오. (필요 시 단어를 추가할 것)

A: Do you know who Mother Teresa was?
B: Of course. She was known as 'An angel of the poor' ⓐ <u>그녀는 가난한 사람들을 도와주었기 때문에</u>. (help, the poor)

→ ______________________________

고난도

24 서술형

〈보기〉의 밑줄 친 if와 쓰임이 같은 것을 모두 고르면?

보기
I don't know <u>if</u> I can pass the entrance exam.

ⓐ <u>If</u> you like it, don't hesitate to buy it.
ⓑ <u>If</u> it snows a lot, let's make a snowman.
ⓒ Please tell me <u>if</u> you gave me this present.
ⓓ They will have dinner <u>if</u> the restaurant is still open.
ⓔ He wonders <u>if</u> his mom will allow him to sleep over at Jack's house.

① ⓑ, ⓔ ② ⓒ, ⓓ ③ ⓒ, ⓔ
④ ⓐ, ⓑ, ⓒ ⑤ ⓐ, ⓒ, ⓔ

고난도

25 서술형 심화

그림을 보고 주어진 〈조건〉에 따라 영작하시오.

(1)

(2)

(1)
조건
1. 다음 어휘를 활용할 것:
tall, the roller coaster, enough to
2. 13단어로 이루어진 완전한 영어 문장으로 쓸 것

나는 내가 이 롤러코스터를 탈 수 있는 충분한 키인지 모르겠어.

→ ______________________________

(2)
조건
1. 다음 어휘를 활용할 것:
not sure, pass, or not, I'm
2. 10단어로 이루어진 완전한 영어 문장으로 쓸 것

나는 시험에 통과했는지 아닌지 확실하지 않다.

→ ______________________________

CHAPTER 07

관계사

관계사

관계사는 절 (「주어 + 동사 ~」)을 이끌어 명사를 뒤에서 꾸며주는 말이다. 관계사에는 「접속사 + 대명사」의 역할을 하는 **관계대명사**와 「접속사 + 부사」의 역할을 하는 **관계부사**가 있다.

- **접속사의 쓰임**

관계대명사: 「접속사+대명사」의 역할	I watched a thriller movie, and it was very interesting. → I watched a thriller movie [which[that] was very interesting]. 나는 매우 재미있는 공포 영화를 보았다.
관계부사: 「접속사+부사(구)」의 역할	New York is the city. We first met in the city. → New York is the city [where we first met]. 뉴욕은 우리가 처음 만났던 도시이다.

한눈에 쏙! 문법 Chart

	선행사	사람	사물/동물	사람/사물/동물
관계대명사의 종류	주격	who	which	that
	소유격	whose	of which(whose)	whose
	목적격	who(m)	which	that
관계대명사 that만 쓸 때	(1) 선행사가 〈사람 + 사물〉이나 〈사람 + 동물〉일 때 (2) 최상급, 서수, the only(유일한), the very(바로 그), the same(같은), all, every, -thing으로 끝나는 부정대명사 등이 선행사에 있을 때			
관계대명사 what	(1) 관계대명사 what이 이끄는 절 앞에는 명사(선행사)가 없다. (선행사 포함) (2) 관계대명사 what이 이끄는 절: 문장에서 명사처럼 주어, 목적어, 보어 역할을 한다.			
관계대명사의 생략	(1) 목적격 관계대명사는 생략할 수 있다. (2) 「주격관계대명사 + be동사」뒤에 분사(또는 형용사)가 올 때, 「주격관계대명사 + be동사」는 생략할 수 있다.			
「전치사 + 관계대명사」	관계대명사는 목적격이지만 생략할 수 없고, 관계대명사 that으로 바꾸어 쓰지 못한다.			
관계대명사의 용법	(1) 제한적 용법: 관계대명사절이 선행사를 수식하면서 선행사의 의미를 제한한다. (2) 계속적 용법: 관계대명사 앞에 쉼표(,)를 쓴다. (that은 쓸 수 없고, 생략 불가)			
관계부사	where(장소), when(시간), why(이유), how(방법)			
복합관계사	복합관계대명사	who(m)ever(~하는 누구든지), whichever(~하는 것은 어느 것이든지), whatever(~하는 것은 무엇이든지)		
	복합관계부사	whenever(~할 때마다), wherever(~하는 어디에나), however(아무리 ~해도)		

핵심만 쏙! 문법 Point

Point 01 관계대명사는 선행사의 종류에 따라 달라져요!

- **관계대명사**는 「**접속사 + 대명사**」의 역할을 하며, 관계대명사절은 선행사(앞에 나온 명사)를 수식한다.
  This book is about a girl. And she falls in love with a prince.
  → This book is about a girl [who falls in love with a prince]. 이 책은 왕자와 사랑에 빠지는 소녀에 관한 것이다.

- **관계대명사**는 선행사의 종류에 따라 **who**, **which**, **that** 등으로 쓴다.

선행사	사람	사물/동물	사람/사물/동물
주격	who	which	that
소유격	whose	of which(whose)	whose
목적격	who(m)	which	that

  This is the story of a boy who[that] had a creative idea to help others. (선행사: a boy/사람)
  He used old materials which[that] were from the garbage to make useful things. (선행사: old materials/사물)

- **관계대명사 that**의 활용
  (1) **선행사가 〈사람 + 사물〉**이나 **〈사람 + 동물〉**일 때
  A girl and her dog that had disappeared have not been found yet. (선행사: A girl and her dog)
  (2) 최상급, 서수, **the only**(유일한), **the very** (바로 그), **the same** (같은), **all**, **every**, **-thing**으로 끝나는 부정대명사 등이 선행사에 있을 때 관계대명사 that을 쓴다.
  He was the last person that left the room. (선행사: the last person)
  Tell me everything that you saw about the accident. (선행사: everything)
  All that glitters is not gold. (선행사: all)

- **관계대명사 that vs. 접속사 that: 관계대명사 that은 불완전한 문장을 이끌고, 접속사 that은 완전한 문장을 이끈다.**

관계대명사 that	Do you know the girl (that is giving a speech now)? (that절이 명사 the girl을 꾸며주는 형용사 역할) 명사 / that절에 주어가 생략되었음
접속사 that	Did you know (that Susan won the speech contest)? (that절이 동사 know의 목적어) that절에 생략된 문장요소 없음

Point 02 관계대명사 what 앞에는 명사(선행사)가 없어요!

- **관계대명사 what**: 그 자체가 'the thing(s) that'의 뜻으로, **선행사를 포함**한다.
  따라서, 관계대명사 **what**이 이끄는 절 **앞에는 명사(선행사)가 없다.**
  This blouse is what she bought online last week. (what = the thing that)

- **관계대명사 what이 이끄는 절**: 문장에서 명사처럼 주어, 목적어, 보어 역할을 한다.
  관계대명사 what이 이끄는 절이 주어로 쓰이면, 단수로 취급한다는 사실에 유의한다.
  What my brother did today was playing computer games. (주어 역할)
  My mom didn't like what my brother did today. (목적어 역할)
  The truth is what I told you. (보어 역할)

핵심만 콕! 문법 Check

A 괄호 안에서 알맞은 말을 고르시오.

1 I failed the history test (who, which) I took yesterday.
2 Ji-sung Park is the Korean soccer player (which, whom) I admire most.
3 The building (which, whose) walls are all made of glass is the museum.
4 I couldn't believe (that, what) I saw at that time.
5 This is (that, what) I have done in the morning.
6 The little girl gave the thing (that, what) she had in her pocket to me.

B 밑줄 친 부분이 어법상 맞으면 O표, 틀리면 알맞게 고치시오.

1 This is all <u>which</u> she wanted. → ____________
2 This is the very bag <u>which</u> I have been looking for. → ____________
3 John was the first runner <u>who</u> crossed the finish line. → ____________
4 Don't forget to bring the boy and his dog <u>that</u> are waiting for you. → ____________

C 다음 두 문장을 관계대명사를 이용하여 한 문장으로 만드시오.

1 He found a book. It was titled *Using Energy*.
→ He found a book ________________________.

2 Mary made a new friend. She met her at the park.
→ Mary made a new friend ________________________.

3 The woman is my grandmother. Her hair is grey.
→ The woman ________________________ is my grandmother.

D 우리말과 같은 뜻이 되도록 괄호 안의 말을 이용하여 문장을 완성하시오.

1 그가 우리에게 말했던 모든 것은 사실로 판명되었다. (he, told, us, everything, that, had)
→ ________________________ turned out to be true.

2 그는 내가 본 가장 키가 큰 소년이다. (He's, I, have ever seen, the tallest, that, boy)
→ ________________________.

3 오늘 우리가 해야 할 것을 말해 주세요. (should, what, do, we)
→ Tell us ________________________ today.

4 그녀는 내가 집에 오는 길에 본 것을 듣고 놀랐다. (saw, what, I)
→ She was surprised to hear ________________________ on my way home.

Point 03 목적격 관계대명사, 「주격 관계대명사 + be동사」는 생략 가능해요!

- **목적격 관계대명사**는 생략할 수 있다.
  Mr. Smith didn't like the funny story (which) I wrote.
  You are lucky to have friends (whom) you can depend on.

- **「주격관계대명사 + be동사」**뒤에 분사(또는 형용사)가 올 때, **「주격관계대명사 + be동사」**는 생략할 수 있다. 단, 이런 경우에 관계대명사만 생략할 수는 없다.
  The girl (who is) running into the classroom is Amy. (O)
  (who만 생략하는 건 안 됨)

Point 04 목적격 관계대명사 앞에는 전치사가 올 수 있어요!

- **관계대명사가 전치사의 목적어인 경우**는 전치사가 관계대명사 앞으로 올 수 있다.
  단, 이 때의 관계대명사는 **목적격이지만 생략할 수 없고, 관계대명사 that으로 바꾸어 쓰지 못한다.**
  Hana found the book (which/that) she had been looking for. (which/that: 생략 가능)
  = Hana found the book for which she had been looking. (which: 생략 불가)
  cf. Hana found the book for that she had been looking. (X)

Point 05 관계대명사는 선행사를 수식할 때와 추가설명을 할 때가 있어요!

- 관계대명사의 용법

  (1) 제한적 용법: **관계대명사절이 선행사를 수식**하면서 선행사의 의미를 제한한다.
  He has two sons who became singers.
  그에게는 '가수가 된 두 아들'이 있다. (→ 가수가 아닌 다른 자녀가 있을 가능성이 있음)

  (2) 계속적 용법: **선행사에 추가적인 설명을 덧붙일 때 사용**하며, 관계대명사 앞에 쉼표(,)를 쓴다.
  이 경우는 **who와 which**만 **가능**하고 that은 쓸 수 없으며, 생략도 할 수 없다.
  또한 **「접속사 + 대명사」**로 바꿔 쓸 수 있다.
  He has two sons, who became singers.
  그에게는 아들이 두 명 있는데, 그들은 가수가 되었다. (who: that으로 바꿔 쓸 수 없음)
  = He has two sons, and they became singers. (아들이 두 명밖에 없고, 그 둘 다 가수가 되었음)
  My dad took me night fishing, which made me very happy. (which는 이 경우 생략 불가)

- **계속적 용법으로 쓰인 which**: 앞에 나온 구나 절 전체를 가리킬 수 있다.
  He arrived at the station late, which made him miss the train. (앞절 전체를 가리킴)

핵심만 콕! 문법 Check

A 문장에서 생략할 수 있는 부분을 찾아 쓰시오. (생략할 부분이 없으면 X표 하시오.)

1 The first thing that she did was to look around. ______________
2 Science is the subject which he is interested in. ______________
3 The girl whom he is playing with now is my niece. ______________
4 This is the girl who won first place in the competition. ______________
5 Everyone who was paying attention to the teacher noticed it. ______________

B 괄호 안에서 알맞은 말을 모두 고르시오. (필요한 말이 없을 땐, X를 고르시오.)

1 Tom is the boy with (X, who, whom, that) I studied yesterday.
2 That building is the place at (X, which, that) my father is working.
3 This is the candy shop to (X, which, that) Amanda goes every day.
4 I know a nice restaurant (X, which, that) my coworker recommended.
5 The man (X, who, that) is talking with my mom is my uncle.
6 Do you want to see an animal show (X, which, in which, that) tigers are playing?
7 I asked her about the man (X, who, whom, that) she came across on the street.

C 두 문장의 뜻이 같도록 관계대명사를 활용하여 빈칸에 알맞은 말을 쓰시오.

1 She told me her phone number, and I saved it in my cell phone.
→ She told me her phone number, ______________ I saved in my cell phone.

2 She grew up in Seoul, and it is a metropolitan city.
→ She grew up in ______________ a metropolitan city.

3 He brought his friend Jane, and she was from America.
→ He brought ______________ from America.

4 The Eiffel Tower is one of the most popular tourist attractions, and it is in Paris.
→ The Eiffel Tower, ______________, is one of the most popular tourist attractions.

D 우리말과 뜻이 같도록 괄호 안의 말을 바르게 배열하여 문장을 완성하시오

1 꽃을 들고 있는 남자가 Jake이다. (holding, is, flowers)
→ The man ______________ Jake.

2 그녀는 영어로 쓰여진 책을 읽고 있다. (English, in, written)
→ She is reading a book ______________.

핵심만 쏙! 문법 Point

Point 06 관계부사는 「전치사 + 관계대명사」로 바꿔 쓸 수 있어요!

- **관계부사**는 문장에서 「**접속사 + 부사**」의 **역할**을 하며, 선행사에 따라 달라진다.
  관계부사가 이끄는 절은 앞에 나온 명사(선행사)를 수식하는 형용사절이다.
  This is the house. + Mozart was born in the house. 이 곳이 모차르트가 태어난 집이다.
  → This is the house [where Mozart was born].

- **관계부사**는 「**전치사 + 관계대명사**」로 바꿔 쓸 수 있다.

선행사	전치사 + 관계대명사	관계부사
장소 (the place, the city, the country 등)	at[in, on, to] + which	where
시간 (the day, the week, the time 등)	at[in, on, to] + which	when
이유 (the reason)	for which	why
방법 (the way)	in which	how

Point 07 선행사와 절대 함께 쓰지 않는 관계부사가 있어요!

- 관계부사 또는 선행사의 생략: 관계부사의 선행사가 **the time, the place, the reason, the way** 등과 같이 일반적인 것일 때 **관계부사나 선행사 둘 중 하나를 생략**할 수 있다.
  Do you know (the reason) why he dropped out of school?
  This swimming pool is (the place) where the TV drama was shot.
- **선행사 the way와 how는 함께 쓰지 않는다**. 반드시 하나를 생략하거나, how 대신 that을 쓴다.
  She couldn't figure out the way(혹은 how) he solved the problem.
  cf. She couldn't figure out the way how he solved the problem. (X)
- **관계부사의 계속적 용법**: 계속적 용법으로 쓰인 관계부사는 ① 생략할 수 없고, ② 「**접속사 + 부사**」로 바꿔 쓸 수 있다. 단, why와 how는 계속적 용법으로 쓸 수 없다.
  She went to England, where she wrote her famous novel.
  → She went to England, and she wrote her famous novel there.

Point 08 복합관계사는 「관계사 + ~ever」로 써요!

- **복합관계대명사**는 「**관계대명사-ever**」의 형태로, 명사절 또는 양보의 부사절을 이끈다.

복합관계대명사	명사절		양보의 부사절	
whoever	~하는 누구든지	(= anyone who)	누가 ~할 지라도	(= no matter who)
whomever	~하는 누구든지	(= anyone whom)	누구를 ~할 지라도	(= no matter whom)
whichever	~하는 것은 어느 것이든지	(= anything which)	어느 것을 ~할 지라도	(= no matter which)
whatever	~하는 것은 무엇이든지	(= anything that)	무엇을 ~할 지라도	(= no matter what)

  Anyone who comes first will get the prize. 가장 먼저 오는 사람은 누구든지 상을 받을 것이다.
  → Whoever comes first will get the prize. (명사절: 문장의 주어 역할)

- **복합관계부사**는 「**관계부사-ever**」의 형태로 부사절을 이끈다.

복합관계부사	시간, 장소의 부사절		양보의 부사절	
whenever	~할 때마다	(= at any time when)	언제 ~하더라도	(= no matter when)
wherever	~하는 어디에나	(= at any place where)	어디에서 ~하더라도	(= no matter where)
however	–		아무리 ~해도	(= no matter how)

  Call me whenever (= at any time when) you need my help. 내 도움이 필요할 때면 언제든지 전화하세요.
  Wherever (= No matter where) you go, try to follow the rules there. 어디에 가든 거기의 규칙을 따르도록 노력해라.

핵심만 콕! 문법 Check

A

괄호 안에서 알맞은 말을 고르시오.

1 She told me (which, how) she made her cookies.
2 This is the library (which, where) I used to study in.
3 That is the reason (which, why) he failed the test for.
4 Tomorrow is the day (which, when) my midterm tests end.
5 Seoul is the city (which, where) over one fourth of the Korean population lives.
6 April 5th is the day (which, when) people used to have a holiday to plant trees on.

B

다음 두 문장을 한 문장으로 만들 때 빈칸에 알맞은 말을 쓰시오.

1 That was the reason. + She was angry at me for the reason.
→ That was __________ __________ she was angry at me.

2 He showed the way. I could make a model plane in the way.
→ He showed __________ I could make a model plane.

3 Do you know the date? + The great king Sejong was born on that date.
→ Do you know __________ the great king Sejong was born?

4 This restaurant is the place. + You can have Italian food at the restaurant.
→ This restaurant is __________ you can have Italian food.

C

두 문장의 뜻이 같도록 밑줄 친 부분에 유의하여 〈보기〉와 같이 문장을 다시 쓰시오.

> 보기
> No matter what you do, do your best.
> → Whatever you do, do your best.

1 No matter which you choose, I'll give it to you.
→ __________ you choose, I'll give it to you.

2 Invite anyone whom you meet on the street to the feast.
→ Invite __________ you meet on the street to the feast.

3 Anyone who wants to get a good grade has to study hard.
→ __________ wants to get a good grade has to study hard.

D

우리말과 뜻이 같도록 괄호 안의 말과 적절한 복합관계사를 이용하여 문장을 완성하시오.

1 네가 알고 있는 것은 무엇이든지 나에게 말해라. (know)
→ Tell me __________ __________ __________.

2 누가 문을 두드리든 간에 문을 열어주지 말아라. (knock)
→ Don't open the door, __________ __________ on it.

3 아무리 부자라 할지라도 사람들은 만족하지 못한다. (rich, they)
→ People never feel satisfied, __________ __________ __________ __________.

내신 만점! 실전 기출

[1~3] 빈칸에 알맞은 말을 고르시오.

01

The astronaut gave some advice to people __________ want to go into space.

① who ② which ③ whom
④ of which ⑤ whose

02

He said to me, "Break a leg", __________ means "Good luck."

① who ② which ③ whom
④ that ⑤ whose

03

There are many words __________ origins are from names of people.

① who ② that ③ what
④ which ⑤ whose

04 우리말과 뜻이 같도록 빈칸 ⓐ에 알맞은 말은?

ⓐ ________________(아무리 어려울지라도), I will not give up.

① It may be however hard
② It may be hard however
③ However hard it may be
④ However hard may it be
⑤ However it may be hard

[5~6] 빈칸에 공통으로 알맞은 말을 고르시오.

05

(1) Do you know __________ 'doggie bag' means?
(2) She told the police officer __________ she saw.

① who ② that ③ what
④ which ⑤ whom

06

(1) There was a giant elephant in the London Zoo __________ was very popular with children.
(2) He said __________ he felt very pleased when he saw me again.

① who ② that ③ what
④ which ⑤ whom

07 서술형

우리말과 뜻이 같도록 괄호 안의 단어를 활용하여 문장을 완성하시오.

그 박물관에서 우리가 볼 모든 화석들을 상상해 봐!
(imagine, the, see, will, fossils, all, that, we)

→ ____________________________________
____________________ in the museum!

08 서술형

우리말과 뜻이 같도록 빈칸에 알맞은 말을 쓰시오.

네가 무엇을 하든지 항상 최선을 다해라.

→ ____________________ you do, do your best.

09 빈칸에 알맞은 말이 순서대로 바르게 나열된 것은?

- Choose ⓐ __________ color you like.
- ⓑ __________ you come, we will welcome you.

① whichever, Whenever
② whatever, However
③ however, Whenever
④ however, Whichever
⑤ whenever, However

10 밑줄 친 부분의 쓰임이 나머지와 다른 하나는?

① She showed me a backpack that was on sale.
② She said that she prefers waffles to hotdogs.
③ Wear this T-shirt that will make you look fashionable.
④ Would you recommend a book that I can read on the train?
⑤ This is a new model that is very popular among young people.

11 서술형

빈칸 ⓐ, ⓑ에 공통으로 알맞은 말을 쓰시오. (단, 대소문자 무시)

- This is the place ⓐ __________ he found the dog.
- ⓑ __________ can I have my computer repaired?

→ ______________________________

12 다음 문장에서 'who is'가 생략된 곳은?

The boy ① throwing ② a ball ③ is ④ my brother ⑤.

13 서술형

우리말과 뜻이 같도록 괄호 안의 말을 바르게 배열하여 문장을 완성하시오.

나의 삼촌에 의해 보내진 그 책은 정말 재미있었다.
(interesting, sent, my, uncle, was, very, by)

→ The book ______________________________
______________________________.

14 〈보기〉의 밑줄 친 부분과 쓰임이 같은 것은?

보기
I promise that I will do what I can do.

① She asked what 'panic' means.
② What kind of job would you like to have?
③ What I like to do most is to watch movies.
④ He didn't know what he should say at that time.
⑤ I didn't know what to do next to solve the puzzle.

15 서술형

두 문장의 뜻이 같도록 빈칸에 알맞은 말을 써서 문장을 완성하시오.

The expression 'Pandora's box' comes from the Greek myth, and it tells about gods and goddesses.

→ The expression 'Pandora's box' comes from __________ __________ __________, __________ tells about gods and goddesses.

16 서술형

두 문장의 뜻이 같도록 빈칸에 알맞은 말을 쓰시오.

Do you know how he made the windmill?

→ Do you know __________ __________ he made the windmill?

17 빈칸 ⓐ~ⓓ에 알맞은 말이 순서대로 바르게 나열된 것은?

- Is that the hotel ⓐ __________ we will stay tonight?
- That is the reason ⓑ __________ she didn't come early.
- We all remember ⓒ __________ we first won the final match.
- This is the forest through ⓓ __________ people passed to go to the village.

① when, how, when, that
② when, why, when, that
③ where, why, when, which
④ where, why, when, that
⑤ where, how, when, which

18 밑줄 친 부분이 어법상 옳은 것은?

① That is the building on which the bank is.
② This is the locker of which I put my school books.
③ He had a passion with which he made the electric car.
④ Germany is the country in which Hamburgers came.
⑤ I gave my brother a toy by which I paid two thousand won.

19 어법상 어색한 것은?

① That was why she couldn't make it in time.
② This is the way how he solved the riddle so easily.
③ I forgot the place where I put my backpack.
④ There was a time when Korea was a Japanese colony.
⑤ Pyramids are places where many tourists want to go.

20 밑줄 친 부분 중 생략할 수 있는 것은?

① I remember when I first met her.
② Do you know the boy with whom John is talking now?
③ Could you recommend a restaurant that you like most?
④ The movie *Avengers*, which children loved to watch, was very fun.
⑤ The word *paparazzi* means annoying photographers who follow stars.

21 밑줄 친 that이 어법상 옳은 것은?

① People could receive that they needed.
② That he saw in the dark was a big wild dog.
③ This is the book that Mandy wanted to borrow from me.
④ Chocolate ice cream is that she wanted to have for dessert.
⑤ Bill had no money, that stopped him from traveling with us this time.

22 서술형

다음 두 문장을 「전치사 + 관계대명사」를 사용하여 한 문장으로 쓰시오.

Tell me the reason. + You came to class very late for the reason.

→ ______________________________
____

신유형

23 밑줄 친 ⓐ~ⓔ에 대한 설명이 틀린 친구는 누구인가?

There are many ways that ⓐ add new words into languages. One interesting way is using brand names. One example is the word *Kleenex*, ⓑ which comes from the name of a product ⓒ which was made by a tissue company. The company produced a new facial tissue and named it *Kleenex*, ⓓ who became a common name ⓔ people use to refer to any common facial tissue now.

① 은지: ⓐ는 many ways와 수를 일치시킨 거야.
② 민영: ⓑ는 that으로도 쓸 수 있어.
③ 희진: ⓒ는 생략할 수 있어.
④ 민규: ⓓ는 선행사가 사물이니까 which로 써야 해.
⑤ 도현: ⓔ는 목적격 관계대명사가 생략된 거야.

24 빈칸 ⓐ~ⓒ에 알맞은 말을 순서대로 바르게 나열한 것은?

We sweat ⓐ (whenever, whatever) we feel hot, and so do animals. The color of sweat is usually colorless, but a hippo's sweat is red. That's ⓑ (what, that) made people in the past think that hippos sweat blood! However, it actually protects hippo's skin from the sun and helps to heal injured skin. ⓒ (However, Whatever) strange it looks, it actually keeps hippos healthy!

① whatever, that, whatever
② whenever, what, however
③ whatever, what, however
④ whatever, that, however
⑤ whenever, that, whatever

고난도

25 서술형 심화

표의 내용과 일치하도록 관계사를 활용하여 문장을 완성하시오.

Who	What	When
Yeongsil Jang	made a water clock	in 1398
Thomas Edison	invented a light bulb	in 1880

(1) Yeongsil Jang was the person __________ __________ a water clock in 1398.

(2) A light bulb is __________ Thomas Edison __________ in 1880.

CHAPTER 08

가정법

가정법

실제 일어나지 않은 일에 대해 반대로 가정해서 자신의 의견이나 소망을 표현하는 방법이 가정법(假定法)이다. 즉, 거짓으로(假) 정하여(定) 표현하는 방법(法)을 뜻한다. 가정법에는 가정법 과거와 가정법 과거완료가 있으며, 대개 if, I wish, as if 등의 표현과 함께 쓴다.

한눈에 쏙! 문법 Chart

가정법 현재(조건부사절)	현재 또는 미래의 일에 대한 가정 (일어날 가능성이 있음)	If 주어 + 동사의 현재형, 주어 + 조동사의 현재형 + 동사원형
가정법 과거	현재의 사실을 반대로 가정 (일어날 가능성이 거의 없음)	If 주어 + 동사의 과거형, 주어 + 조동사의 과거형 + 동사원형
가정법 과거완료	과거의 사실을 반대로 가정	If 주어 + had p.p., 주어 + 조동사의 과거형 + have p.p.
혼합가정법	과거와 현재를 동시에 반대로 가정 (과거와 현재가 서로 관련 있음)	If 주어 + had p.p., 주어 + 조동사의 과거형 + 동사원형
I wish +가정법 과거	현재나 미래의 실현될 수 없는 소망	I wish 주어 + 동사의 과거형
I wish +가정법 과거완료	과거에 이루지 못한 일에 대한 아쉬움이나 소망	I wish 주어 + had p.p.
as if +가정법 과거	현재의 사실과 반대되는 일	as if 주어 + 동사의 과거형
as if +가정법 과거완료	과거의 사실과 반대되는 일	as if 주어 + had p.p.
if it were not for (만일 ~이 없다면)	현재의 사실을 반대로 가정	= without = but for
if it had not been for (만일 ~이 없었다면)	과거의 사실을 반대로 가정	= without = but for
if 생략	if절에 'were, had, should'등이 오면 접속사 if를 생략하고 주어와 동사를 도치	If it were not for → Were it not for If it had not been for → Had it not been for

핵심만 쏙! 문법 Point

Point 01 가정법 과거는 현재 사실과 반대되거나 이루어질 가능성이 낮은 일을 가정할 때 써요!

- **가정법 과거**는 **현재 사실과 반대**되거나 **이루어질 가능성이 낮은 일**을 가정할 때 쓴다.

「If + 주어 + 동사의 과거형/were ~, 주어 + 조동사의 과거형 + 동사원형 …」'만일 ~라면, …할 텐데'
would/could/should/might

- **가정법 과거 → 직설법 현재 전환 방법**: 과거시제는 현재시제로 바꾸고, 긍정은 부정으로, 부정은 긍정으로 바꾼다. If는 접속사 as, so, because로 바꿔 쓴다.
  If we had wings, we could fly. 만약 우리에게 날개가 있다면, 우리는 날 수 있을 텐데. (가정법 과거)
  → As we don't have wings, we can't fly. 우리에게 날개가 없어서 날 수 없다. (직설법 현재)

- 가정법 과거에서 **If절의 동사가 be동사일 경우**, 주어의 인칭이나 수에 상관없이 **were**를 쓴다.
  If I were you, I would buy that blouse. 만약 내가 너라면, 그 블라우스를 살 텐데.

Point 02 가정법 과거는 현재 사실과 반대되거나 이루어질 가능성이 낮은 일을 가정할 때 써요!

- **가정법 과거완료**는 **과거 사실과 반대**되거나 **이루어질 가능성이 낮은 일**을 가정할 때 쓴다.

「If + 주어 + had p.p. ~, 주어 + 조동사의 과거형 + have p.p. …」'만일 ~했다면, …했을 텐데'
would/could/should/might

- **가정법 과거완료 → 직설법 과거 전환 방법**: 과거완료는 과거로 바꾸고, 긍정은 부정으로, 부정은 긍정으로 바꾼다. If는 접속사 as, so, because로 바꿔 쓴다.
  If she had won the game, she would have been happy. (가정법 과거완료)
  만약 그녀가 게임에서 이겼다면, 그녀는 행복했을 텐데.
  → As she didn't win the game, she wasn't happy. (직설법 과거)
  그녀가 게임에서 이기지 않았기 때문에, 그녀는 행복하지 않았다.

  If I had arrived on time, I wouldn't have missed the class. (가정법 과거완료)
  만약 내가 제 시간에 도착했다면, 나는 수업에 빠지지 않았을 텐데.
  → As I didn't arrive on time, I missed the class. (직설법 과거)
  내가 제 시간에 도착하지 않아서, 나는 수업에 빠졌다.

핵심만 콕! 문법 Check

A 괄호 안에서 알맞은 말을 고르시오.

1 If I (was, were) 10 years younger, I would study harder.
2 If the ring (were not, is not) so expensive, he would buy it.
3 If my dad were here, he (will allow, would allow) me to go out.
4 If the boy were 130cm tall, he (can, could) ride the roller coaster.
5 If she had enough money, she (would go, would have gone) on a trip to Europe.

B 밑줄 친 동사의 시제를 어법에 맞게 고쳐 쓰시오.

1 If he had seen the movie, he would <u>like</u> it a lot. → ____________
2 If a policeman <u>saw</u> her, he would have caught her. → ____________
3 If she <u>knew</u> about the exhibition, she would have gone there. → ____________
4 If the people had behaved well, there <u>wouldn't be</u> a big fight. → ____________
5 If the girl <u>hasn't had</u> her hair permed, she would have looked prettier. → ____________

C 두 문장의 뜻이 같도록 빈칸에 알맞은 말을 쓰시오.

1 As Tony doesn't know the problem, he can't solve it.
→ If ____________________, he could solve it.

2 As I'm not in your shoes, I won't accept the offer.
→ If ____________________, I would accept the offer.

3 If the weather had been warm, they would have swum in the sea.
→ As ______________ warm, they ______________ in the sea.

4 If I had studied hard, I could have gotten a good score.
→ As ______________ hard, I ______________ a good score.

D 우리말과 뜻이 같도록 괄호 안의 말을 바르게 배열하여 문장을 완성하시오.

1 만약 그가 약속이 없다면, 그는 좀 쉴 텐데. (didn't, if, have, he, he, would, an appointment)
→ ______________________________ get some rest.

2 만약 내가 아침밥을 먹었더라면, 나는 배고프지 않았을 텐데.
(if, breakfast, I, had, had, I, been, have, wouldn't)
→ ______________________________ hungry.

3 만약 내가 다시 태어난다면, 나는 유명한 가수가 될 텐데. (born, if, were, I, would, I, become, again)
→ ______________________________ a famous singer.

4 만약 그가 연습을 많이 했었다면, 그는 경기에서 이길 수 있었을 텐데.
(he, if, had, a lot, he, practiced, would, won, have)
→ ______________________________ the game.

핵심만 쏙! 문법 Point

Point 03 「I wish + 가정법 과거/과거완료」로 현재나 과거의 사실과 반대인 소망을 나타내요!

- 「I wish + 가정법 과거」는 현재나 미래의 실현될 수 없는 소망이나, 현재 사실에 대한 유감을 나타낸다.

  「I wish + 주어 + 동사의 과거형 ~.」 → 「I am sorry (that) + 주어+ 동사의 현재형」 (직설법 현재)

  I wish I had a new cell phone. → I am sorry (that) I don't have a new cell phone.

- 「I wish + 가정법 과거완료」는 과거에 이루지 못한 일에 대한 아쉬움이나 소망을 나타낼 때 쓴다.

  「I wish + 주어 + had p.p. ~.」 → 「I'm sorry (that) + 주어 + 동사의 과거형」 (직설법 과거)

  I wish I had studied English hard. → I am sorry (that) I didn't study English hard.

Point 04 「as if + 가정법 과거/과거완료」로 현재와 과거 사실의 반대를 나타내요!

- 「as if + 가정법 과거」(마치 ~인 것처럼): 주어 + 동사의 현재/과거형 + as if + 주어 + 동사의 과거
  (1) 주절 동사가 현재일 때: 현재 사실과 반대되는 일 (가정법 과거 → 직설법 현재)
  She **acts** as if she were a famous singer.
  → In fact, she is not a famous singer.
  (2) 주절 동사가 과거일 때: 과거 사실과 반대되는 일 (가정법 과거 → 직설법 과거)
  She **acted** as if she were a famous singer.
  → In fact, she was not a famous singer.
- 「as if + 가정법 과거완료」(마치 ~이었던 것처럼): 주어 + 동사의 현재/과거형 + as if + 주어 + had p.p.
  (1) 주절 동사가 현재일 때: 과거 사실과 반대되는 일 (가정법 과거완료 → 직설법 과거)
  He **sings** as if he had been a singer. → In fact, he was not a singer.
  (2) 주절 동사가 과거일 때: 과거보다 더 앞서 일어난 사실과 반대되는 일 (가정법 과거완료 → 직설법 과거완료)
  She **talked** as if she had been to New York. → In fact, she had not been to New York.

Point 05 without과 but for는 「if it were not for」 혹은 「if it had not been for」와 바꿔 쓸 수 있어요!

- **if it were not for** (만약 ~가 없다면) = **but for = without**
  if it had not been for (만약 ~가 없었다면) = **but for = without**
  If it were not for you, I could not win a gold medal.
  → Without[But for] you, I could not win a gold medal.
  If it had not been for a helping hand, the baby could not have received treatment.
  → Without[But for] a helping hand, the baby could not have received treatment.

Point 06 주의해야 할 가정법

- **가정법 과거/과거완료에서 if절에 'were, had, should'** 등이 오면, **접속사 if를 생략**하고 **주어와 동사를 도치**시킬 수 있다.
  If I were a magician, I would fly home. → Were I a magician, I would fly home.
- **혼합가정법**: 과거의 일이 현재까지 영향을 끼칠 때 사용하며 '(과거에) ~했다면 (지금) ~할 텐데'라는 뜻으로, **if절에는 가정법 과거완료를, 주절에는 가정법 과거를** 쓴다.
  If I had studied harder yesterday, I could answer all these questions now.

핵심만 콕! 문법 Check

A 밑줄 친 부분을 괄호 안의 지시대로 어법에 맞게 고쳐 쓰시오.

1 I wish I <u>can</u> fly like a bird. (I wish 가정법과거) → ____________

2 I wish it <u>have not been</u> raining so hard. (I wish 가정법과거완료) → ____________

3 I wish he <u>was able to</u> speak Chinese well. (I wish 가정법과거) → ____________

4 I wish you <u>had solve</u> the math problems. (I wish 가정법과거완료) → ____________

B 괄호 안에서 알맞은 말을 고르시오.

1 (With, Without) salt, no food could be tasty.

2 If you are busy, I (will, would) ask Tony to help me.

3 He talks as if he (knew, knows) the singer, but he doesn't.

4 But for his great effort, he (can, could) not have passed the test.

5 She speaks English as if she (is, were) a native speaker, but she isn't.

6 If she (is, were) his mom, she could ask him to help the house chores.

C 두 문장의 뜻이 같도록 빈칸에 알맞은 말을 쓰시오.

1 I am sorry that I don't have enough time.
→ I wish ____________________.

2 James practices hard ____________________.
→ In fact, he is not a main actor.

3 If it had not been for the song, she could not have become famous.
→ ____________ the song, she could not have become famous.

4 If they had practiced harder, they could have been the winners.
→ ____________, they could have been the winners.

D 우리말과 같은 뜻이 되도록 괄호 안의 말을 이용하여 문장을 완성하시오.

1 그가 그곳에 갈 수 있다면 좋을 텐데. (go, could, there)
→ I wish he ____________________.

2 그녀는 마치 건강을 회복했던 것처럼 보였다. (as, had, if, she, well, gotten)
→ She looked ____________________.

3 만약 내가 너라면, 나는 더 많이 공부할 텐데. (were, would, I, you, if, study)
→ ____________, I ____________ more.

4 만약 법이 없다면, 우리 사회는 위험할 것이다. (be, the laws, for, would, but)
→ ____________, our society ____________ dangerous.

5 만약 그가 다치지 않았더라면, 그는 훌륭한 축구 선수가 되었을 텐데.
(have, if, been, injured, he, not, would, had, been)
→ ____________, he ____________ a great soccer player.

내신 만점! 실전 기출

[1~2] 빈칸 ⓐ, ⓑ에 알맞은 말이 순서대로 바르게 나열된 것을 고르시오.

01

만약 내가 외계인을 만난다면, 나는 도망갈 거야.
→ If I ⓐ __________ an alien, I ⓑ __________ away.

① meet, run ② meet, ran ③ met, run
④ met, will run ⑤ met, would run

02

If she ⓐ __________ her favorite actor last night, she ⓑ __________ very happy.

① sees, will be
② saw, would be
③ saw, would been
④ has seen, would have been
⑤ had seen, would have been

03 서술형

괄호 안의 단어를 활용하여 빈칸에 알맞은 말을 쓰시오. (필요 시 단어의 형태 변화 가능)

(1) If he __________ rich, he could buy the sports car. (be)
(2) If I __________ a laptop computer, I would lend it to you. (have)
(3) If she had strawberries, she could __________ a strawberry cake. (make)

(1) __________, (2) __________, (3) __________

04 서술형

주어진 질문에 영어로 답하시오.

Q: If you saw a bear on a mountain, what would you do?

→ A: ______________________________

[5~6] 두 문장의 뜻이 같도록 빈칸에 알맞은 말을 쓰시오.

05 서술형

If the brakes worked, the car could stop quickly in time.

→ __________ the brakes __________ __________, the car __________ stop quickly in time.

06 서술형

As I am so tired, I cannot go with them.

→ If __________ __________ __________ so tired, I __________ __________ with them.

07 빈칸에 알맞은 말은?

그는 마치 아무것도 모르는 것처럼 말하는데, 그것은 사실이 아니다.
→ He talks as if he __________ nothing, which is not true.

① know ② knew ③ knows
④ knowing ⑤ had known

08 빈칸 ⓐ, ⓑ에 알맞은 말이 차례대로 짝지어진 것은?

그것은 마치 그 영화가 신기록을 세웠었던 것처럼 들린다.
→ It sounds ⓐ __________ the movie ⓑ __________ a new record.

① as if, sets ② as if, set
③ even if, has set ④ as if, had set
⑤ even if, had set

09 서술형

세 문장이 같은 뜻이 되도록 빈칸에 알맞은 말을 쓰시오.

> Without the Internet, we could not get information so easily.

→ (1) ________ ________ the Internet, we ________ ________ ________ information so easily.

→ (2) If it ________ ________ ________ the internet, we ________ ________ ________ information so easily.

10 다음 밑줄 친 문장과 의미가 같은 것은?

> My friends and I were going to play baseball yesterday but we couldn't because it rained a lot. I'm sorry that it rained cats and dogs.

① I wish it will rain cats and dogs.
② I wish it was rained cats and dogs.
③ I wish it had rained cats and dogs.
④ I wish it hadn't rained cats and dogs.
⑤ I wish it haven't rained cats and dogs.

11 문맥에 맞도록 밑줄 친 우리말을 영어로 바르게 옮긴 것은?

> I made a rule to exercise every day at the beginning of this year, but I haven't kept the rule. These days, I get sick easily because I don't exercise. 만일 내가 규칙적으로 운동한다면 건강을 유지할 수 있을 텐데.

① If I exercised regularly, I can stay healthy.
② If I exercised regularly, I can't stay healthy.
③ If I exercised regularly, I could stay healthy.
④ If I didn't exercised regularly, I could stay healthy.
⑤ If I don't exercise regularly, I couldn't stay healthy.

12 서술형

〈보기〉를 참고하여 빈칸에 알맞은 말을 쓰시오.

> 보기
>
> Sally는 마치 대학생인 것처럼 공부한다.
> (university student)
> → Sally studies as if she were a university student.

> 재민이는 마치 원어민인 것처럼 영어를 말한다.
> (native speaker)

→ Jaemin speaks English ______________________ .

최다빈출

[13~14] 짝지어진 두 문장의 의미가 다른 것을 고르시오.

13

① If he were free, he could join us.
→ As he wasn't free, he can't join us.
② If it were not cold, they could go hiking.
→ As it is cold, they can't go hiking.
③ If I had money, I could buy the ring.
→ As I don't have money, I can't buy the ring.
④ If I were hungry, I could finish all the food.
→ As I am not hungry, I can't finish all the food.
⑤ If she told me the truth, I could trust her.
→ As she doesn't tell me the truth, I can't trust her.

14

① If he were fine, he could go to the movies.
= As he isn't fine, he can't go to the movies.
② If I were not exhausted, I could play outside.
= I'm exhausted, so I can't play outside.
③ If there were no traffic, we could arrive on time.
= Because there is traffic, we can't arrive on time.
④ If she were from the U.S., she could speak English fluently.
= As she isn't from the U.S., she can speak English fluently.
⑤ If she knew Dr. Jackson's phone number, she would call and ask him.
= As she doesn't know Dr. Jackson's phone number, she can't call and ask him.

15 괄호 안에서 알맞은 단어를 차례대로 나열한 것은?

- I wish he ⓐ (has, had, have) not left me alone.
- I wish she ⓑ (can, could) sing well.

① have, could ② have, can ③ had, could
④ had, can ⑤ has, could

16 주어진 문장과 의미가 같은 것을 고르시오.

If she knew the password, she could open the door.

① She knew the password, so she could open the door.
② As she didn't know the password, she can't open the door.
③ She doesn't know the password, so she can open the door.
④ As she doesn't know the password, she can't open the door.
⑤ As she doesn't know the password, she couldn't open the door.

17 서술형

두 문장의 뜻이 같도록 빈칸에 알맞은 말을 쓰시오.

(A) In fact, they do not know each other.

→ They look ________ ________ they ________ each other.

(B) In fact, they are the owners of this house.

→ My grandparents act ________ ________ they ________ ________ the owners of this house.

18 서술형

〈보기〉와 같이 괄호 안의 말을 활용하여 우리말을 완전한 영어 문장으로 바꿔 쓰시오.

보기

세상의 모든 질병이 치료될 수 있다면 좋을 텐데.
(all kinds of diseases, curable)
→ I wish all diseases in the world were curable.

내가 전과목 만점을 받으면 좋을 텐데.
(get, straight A's)

→ ______________________________
____

19 어법상 옳은 문장은?

① If I had gotten up earlier, I would had not been late.
② If she has read the letter, she would have been glad.
③ If he had spoke Chinese well, she would have hired him.
④ If the rumor had been true, people would have criticized the actor.
⑤ If they had asked the boy his contact number yesterday, they could called him now.

최다빈출

20 어법상 옳지 않은 문장은?

① If he were here, I would ask him for help.
② If I sang well, I would join the singing club.
③ If you give him this letter, I will really appreciate it.
④ If I had enough money, I could have bought a house.
⑤ If she were not busy, she could play softball with her friends.

21 서술형

주어진 우리말을 〈조건〉에 따라 영작하시오.

조건
1. 다음 단어를 모두 사용할 것: finish, go, could
2. 필요하면 단어의 형태를 변형할 수 있음.

내가 아침에 숙제를 끝냈더라면, 지금 영화를 보러 갈 수 있을 텐데.

→ ______ ______ ______ ______ my homework in the morning, I ______ ______ to see a movie now.

고난도

22 어법상 어색한 문장을 모두 고르면?

ⓐ If I am you, I would accept his apology.
ⓑ If we had no friends, we would feel lonely.
ⓒ If she had a cell phone now, she would have lent it to him.
ⓓ If you read a lot of books, you could become wiser.
ⓔ If I have no homework today, I could go to the party.

① ⓐ, ⓒ ② ⓒ, ⓔ ③ ⓑ, ⓒ, ⓔ
④ ⓐ, ⓓ, ⓔ ⑤ ⓐ, ⓒ, ⓔ

신유형

23 서술형

대화를 읽고 밑줄 친 우리말 ⓐ와 같은 뜻이 되도록 빈칸에 알맞은 말을 쓰시오.

A: Do you know any famous sayings?
B: Yes, I do know one and it is my motto.
A: What is it?
B: It's what Steve Jobs said in his speech. He said, 'ⓐ 오늘을 인생의 마지막 날인 것처럼 살아라'.

= Live today ______ ______ it ______ the last day of your life.

24 서술형

밑줄 친 ⓐ를 가정법 문장으로 바꿔 쓸 때, 조건에 맞춰 영작하시오.

조건
1. 과거 사실에 반대되는 가정법을 사용할 것.
2. 다음 단어를 활용하여, 총 14단어로 영작할 것: work hard, become, the Sales Queen
3. 부정어는 축약형을 사용하지 말 것.

Thanks to Belle's talent, she was very good at sales. As she was very polite and friendly, people bought new cars from her. She was even selected as the 'Salesperson of the Year' for 2015. ⓐ As she worked so hard, she could become the Sales Queen. So she decided to work much harder.

→ ______________________________

____

고난도

25 서술형 심화

그림을 보고 괄호 안의 말을 활용하여 가정법 과거 문장을 완성하시오. (필요하면 단어의 형태를 바꾸거나 추가)

(1)

(2)

(1) My mom and I were going to go to the zoo today, but now we can't. It is raining too much!
→ If it ______________________________,
______________________________.
(be, sunny, we, can, go, the zoo)

(2) It is my birthday today, but nobody seems to remember it. I am very sad.
→ I wish ______________________________
______________ with my friends.
(have a birthday party, can)

MEMO

부록

A. 불규칙동사 변화표

B. 자주 쓰이는 동명사 표현

C. by 이외의 전치사를 사용하는 수동태 표현

D. 자주 쓰이는 상관접속사 표현

A. 불규칙동사 변화표

원형	과거형	과거분사형	뜻
arise	arose	arisen	생겨나다
awake	awoke	awoken	깨어나다
bear	bore	born	참다, 낳다
become	became	become	~가 되다
begin	began	begun	시작하다
behold	beheld	beheld	주시하다
bend	bent	bent	구부리다
bite	bit	bitten	물다
blow	blew	blown	폭파하다
break	broke	broken	깨다
bring	brought	brought	가져오다
build	built	built	짓다
burn	burnt	burnt	태우다
buy	bought	bought	사다
catch	caught	caught	잡다
choose	chose	chosen	고르다
cost	cost	cost	(값이) ~들다
cut	cut	cut	자르다
deal	dealt	dealt	다루다
dig	dug	dug	파다
draw	drew	drawn	그리다, 당기다
drink	drank	drunk	마시다
drive	drove	driven	운전하다
fall	fell	fallen	떨어지다
feed	fed	fed	먹이다

원형	과거형	과거분사형	뜻
feel	felt	felt	느끼다
fight	fought	fought	싸우다
find	found	found	발견하다
flee	fled	fled	도망치다
fly	flew	flown	날다
forbid	forbade	forbidden	금지하다
forget	forgot	forgotten	잊다
forgive	forgave	forgiven	용서하다
found	founded	founded	설립하다
freeze	froze	frozen	얼리다
get	got	gotten/got	얻다
give	gave	given	주다
grow	grew	grown	자라다
hang	hung	hung	매달다
have	had	had	가지다, 먹다
hear	heard	heard	듣다
hide	hid	hidden	숨기다
hit	hit	hit	치다
hold	held	held	잡다, 개최하다
hurt	hurt	hurt	부상 입히다
keep	kept	kept	유지하다
know	knew	known	알다
lay	laid	laid	놓다
lead	led	led	이끌다
lean	leaned/leant	leaned/leant	기울다

원형	과거형	과거분사형	뜻
leave	left	left	떠나다
lend	lent	lent	빌려주다
let	let	let	놓다
lie	lied	lied	거짓말하다
lie	lay	lain	눕다
light	lit	lit	밝히다
lose	lost	lost	잃다
make	made	made	만들다
mean	meant	meant	의미하다
meet	met	met	만나다
mistake	mistook	mistaken	실수하다
outrun	outran	outrun	앞지르다
overcome	overcame	overcome	극복하다
pay	paid	paid	지불하다
prove	proved	proved/proven	증명하다
put	put	put	놓다
raise	raised	raised	~를 올리다
read	read	read	읽다
ride	rode	ridden	타다
ring	rang	rung	종을 울리다
rise	rose	risen	오르다
run	ran	run	뛰다
say	said	said	말하다
see	saw	seen	보다
sell	sold	sold	팔다

원형	과거형	과거분사형	뜻
send	sent	sent	보내다
set	set	set	정하다
shake	shook	shaken	흔들다
shut	shut	shut	닫다
sing	sang	sung	노래하다
sit	sat	sat	앉다
sleep	slept	slept	자다
slide	slid	slid	미끄러지다
spend	spent	spent	소비하다
spill	spilt	spilt	엎지르다
split	split	split	쪼개다
spoil	spoiled/spoilt	spoiled/spoilt	망치다
spread	spread	spread	퍼지다
stand	stood	stood	서다
steal	stole	stolen	훔치다
swear	swore	sworn	맹세하다
sweep	swept	swept	싹 쓸다
take	took	taken	가지고 가다
teach	taught	taught	가르치다
tear	tore	torn	찢다
tell	told	told	말하다
think	thought	thought	생각하다
wake	woke	woken	깨우다
wear	wore	worn	입다
write	wrote	written	쓰다

B. 자주 쓰이는 동명사 표현

look forward to -ing	~할 것을 고대하다	go -ing	~하러 가다
How[What] about -ing?	~하는 게 어때?	spend *A* (on) -ing	~하는 데 A를 쓰다
be used to -ing	~하는 데에 익숙하다	be busy -ing	~하느라 바쁘다
can't help -ing	~하지 않을 수 없다	have trouble -ing	~하는데 어려움을 겪다
keep[stop] *A* from -ing	*A*를 ~못하게 하다	feel like -ing	~하고 싶다
there is no -ing	~은 불가능하다	on -ing	~하자마자
It is no use -ing	~해도 소용없다	be worth -ing	~할 가치가 있다

C. by 이외의 전치사를 사용하는 수동태 표현

be ashamed of	~을 부끄러워하다	be known for	~로 유명하다
be based on	~에 근거를 두다	be known to	~에게 알려지다
be bored with	~에 지겨워지다	be made from	~로 만들어지다 (재료의 성질 변화)
be covered with	~으로 덮여 있다	be made of	~로 만들어지다 (재료의 모양 변화)
be composed of	~으로 구성되다	be pleased with	~에 기쁘다
be crowded with	~으로 혼잡하다	be satisfied with	~에 만족하다
be disappointed with	~하지 않을 수 없다	be shocked at	~에 충격을 받다
be filled with	~으로 가득 차다	be surprised by(at)	~에 놀라다
be interested in	~에 관심이 있다	be tired of	~에 싫증나다
be known as	~로서 알려지다	be worried about	~에 대해 걱정하다

D. 자주 쓰이는 상관접속사 표현

상관접속사 종류	의미	주어로 올 때 동사의 수 일치
both *A* and *B*	*A*와 *B* 둘 다	동사의 복수형을 취함
not *A* but *B*	*A*가 아닌 *B*	동사의 수는 *B*에 일치
either *A* or *B*	*A*나 *B* 둘 중 하나	
neither *A* nor *B*	*A*도 *B*도 아닌	
not only *A* but also *B*	*A*뿐만 아니라 *B*도	
B as well as *A*		

MEMO

MEMO

단기간에 마무리하는 8가지 핵심 비법

woongjin compass

비법 담은 중학 영문법

Answer Key

특강편 3

단기간에 마무리하는 8가지 핵심 비법

woongjin compass

비법 담은 중학 영문법

Answer Key

특강편 3

Chapter 01 시제

핵심만 콕! 문법 Check

Point 1, 2

A 1. saves 2. did 3. goes 4. is 5. leaves 6. was

B 1. were you 2. did you find 3. O 4. has taught 5. gained 6. has been celebrated

C 1. has, finished 2. has been 3. has gone 4. have been 5. has been

Point 3-5

A 1. had left 2. were 3. feel 4. will be 5. have 6. know 7. are

B 1. had 2. do you think 3. O 4. will be having 또는 will have 5. O

C 1. had received
2. has been swimming
3. had been eating
4. have you been watching
5. has been working

내신 만점! 실전 기출

01. ⑤ **02.** ⑤ **03.** ① **04.** ③
05. ③ **06.** ② **07.** ③ **08.** ③
09. ② **10.** has been
11. has been learning **12.** ③ **13.** ③
14. ① **15.** ③ **16.** ④
17. had, left **18.** Have, heard, sees **19.** ④
20. have finished, will have finished
21. is really resembling, really resembles
22. ④ **23.** ② **24.** ④
25. (1) has got (2) has been reading (3) for five hours

Chapter 02 to부정사

핵심만 콕! 문법 Check

Point 1, 2

A 1. what 2. It 3. when 4. to drive 5. to play with 6. something to give

B 1. ⓑ 의무 2. ⓒ 가능 3. ⓔ 운명 4. ⓒ 보어 5. ⓑ 목적어 6. ⓐ 주어

C 1. am to ride 2. were to fall 3. are to submit

D 1. to make comic books
2. to go backpacking around the world
3. It is time to study
4. is to be held

Point 3-5

A 1. to see 2. for 3. not to be 4. of 5. so as to learn

B 1. not to miss the train
2. decided not to attend the meeting
3. impossible for me

C 1. order not to fail, as not to fail
2. seems to be
3. It seemed that, had been

D 1. to tell the truth
2. to help the poor children there

E 1. very happy to win
2. to swim in the deep sea
3. not to fail
4. seems to have had fun

Point 6-8

A 1. dance 2. to study 3. be
4. to buy 5. to finish

B 1. to study 2. help
3. burn(burning) 4. too hot to drink
5. cry(crying) 6. (to) move

C 1. strong that he can
2. smart that she could
3. shy that she(he) can't
4. small that it can't

D 1. allowed his son to play
2. had the waiter bring
3. too cold to go
4. fast enough to win
5. felt someone stare at

내신 만점! 실전 기출

01. ④ **02.** ① **03.** to become
04. ③ **05.** how to play the flute **06.** ③
07. to hate her children's bad habits **08.** ①
09. (1) be proud of himself(herself)
(2) he(she) is proud of himself(herself)
10. ③ **11.** ③
12. Her parents are so poor that they can't pay her school tuition. **13.** ①
14. when to meet(see) my older sister(her)
15. ③, ④ **16.** She asked him to eat together.
17. ② **18.** ⑤ **19.** ② **20.** ④
21. ③
22. (1) had me feed the dog
(2) asked me to take care of my brother
23. is important for him to practice as much as possible
24. (1) for you -> of you (2) of him -> for him
(3) O (4) of her -> for her
(5) O (6) O
25. (1) asked him to wash the dishes
(2) how to get to the bank
(3) difficult for me to answer

Chapter 03 동명사

핵심만 콕! 문법 Check

Point 1-3

A 1. is 2. Being, To be
3. correcting, to correct 4. working
5. inviting 6. my, me
7. her

B 1. O 2. meeting
3. making 4. his(him) not cleaning

C 1. being late 2. doing 3. her being
4. not missing 5. my(me) having given

Point 4-6

A 1. to stop 2. waiting 3. to go
4. playing 5. talking 6. to open
7. to buy 8. drinking 9. leaving

B 1. O 2. to visit 3. O
4. listening 5. studying 6. laughing
7. finding

C 1. loves climbing 2. wants to start
3. looking forward to going
4. is no use crying

내신 만점! 실전 기출

01. ② **02.** ③ **03.** ① **04.** ④
05. ④ **06.** ④ **07.** ④
08. looking forward to taking **09.** ②
10. ② **11.** ① **12.** ⑤
13. not finding **14.** having missed
15. ④ **16.** ②, ③ **17.** in, from
18. to fish, fishing **19.** ⑤
20. getting tired of wearing
21. ④ **22.** ⑤ **23.** ③
24. Caring about how they look
25. (1) to raise your hand
(2) Using a cell phone
(3) talking with your friends

Chapter 04 분사

핵심만 콕! 문법 Check

Point 1-4

A 1. rising 2. filled
3. made 4. playing

B 1. stole 2. O
3. pleased 4. writing

C 1. fascinating 2. confused
3. touched 4. bored

D 1. novels written by this author
2. the shocking news from our teacher
3. always crowded with many visitors

Point 5-8

A 1. spending money
2. Having studied hard

B 1. Because 2. After

C 1. Being 2. Having been

D 1. Having spent all her money
2. (Having been) Impressed by her music
3. Having got a good score on the test

Point 9-13

A 1. being, were
2. had seen, had not(hadn't) seen

B 1. Not feeling hungry
2. There being no bus so late at night

C 1. with his eyes closed
2. with his arms folded

D 1. Judging from 2. Frankly speaking

내신 만점! 실전 기출

01. ③ **02.** The man riding a wheelchair
03. ② **04.** ④ **05.** ③
06. blocking the narrow road to my house
07. ③ **08.** ③ **09.** ④ **10.** ②, ④
11. ②
12. (Because) Not having brought my wallet
13. ④ **14.** Because she has many friends
15. Not knowing how to solve the problem
16. ④ **17.** ③ **18.** ②, ④ **19.** ③
20. ④ **21.** ②
22. ⓑ, There being no one around me, I couldn't ask for help.
23. ⑤
24. with her eyes fixed on the board
25. (1) Getting first prize in the contest
(2) waving his hand to his friends
(3) Holding her baby in her arms

Chapter 05 수동태

핵심만 콕! 문법 Check

Point 1-4

A 1. released 2. resembles
3. happened 4. prepare

B 1. was criticized 2. was delayed
3. was painted

C 1. can be solved 2. will be shown
3. must be returned

D 1. The school trip was called off by the teacher.
2. Their baby is taken care of by them.
3. He is looked up to by many people in his country.

Point 5-8

A 1. are being cut 2. is not being
3. been cleaned 4. been

B 1. has been organized
2. has been taught

C 1. was given some allowances by his mom
2. were given to Peter by his mom

D 1. come, to come 2. to Nabi, Nabi
3. starting, start 4. buying, to buy

Point 9-12

A 1. to sing 2. to help 3. allowed

B 1. were seen to break
2. were made to do

C 1. It is supposed that his movie is great.
His movie is supposed to be great.
2. It is said that eating an apple a day keeps a doctor away.
Eating an apple a day is said to keep a doctor away.

D 1. known to 2. based on

내신 만점! 실전 기출

01. ③ **02.** ④ **03.** ① **04.** ②
05. should change, should be changed **06.** ⑤
07. ③ **08.** ② **09.** ⑤ **10.** ④
11. was called captain by everyone in his class
12. (1) was offered a great opportunity by his teacher
(2) was offered to him by his teacher
13. ④ **14.** ⑤ **15.** ③
16. (1) is said to be one of the best soccer players
(2) is said that Ji-sung Park is one of the best soccer players
17. ② **18.** ②, ③ **19.** be
20. ④ **21.** ⑤ **22.** ①
23. is looked up to by many people
24. ⑤ **25.** (1) ate, eaten (4) turn, turned

Chapter 06 접속사

핵심만 콕! 문법 Check

Point 1

A 1. to 2. that 3. Whether
4. Since 5. that 6. As 7. while

B 1. 나는 엄마가 집에 있는지 없는지 모르겠다.
2. 그는 버스가 언제 도착하는지 물었다.
3. 나는 타이타닉 영화가 재미있고 로맨틱해서 세 번이나 보았다.
4. 그는 겨우 4살임에도 불구하고 그의 이름을 깔끔하게 쓸 수 있다.

C 1. soft to
2. order to communicate with people

D 1. when the party is
2. if(whether) the people were safe

E 1. that the rumor is true
2. so fast that I couldn't
3. tell me where the post office is

Point 2-4

A 1. nor 2. and 3. but
4. or 5. but

B 1. If you take public transportation
2. If you don't run, Unless you run

C 1. Moreover 2. However 3. Therefore

D 1. neither beef nor pork
2. In addition, she is smart
3. or the sleeping baby will wake up
4. either a lawyer or a police officer
5. and your dreams will come true

내신 만점! 실전 기출

01. ②	02. ①	03. ③	04. ③
05. ②	06. As	07. ⑤	08. ③
09. ②, ⑤	10. ④	11. that	12. ④

13. whether they will do well 14. ③
15. order not to
16. ⓐ until ⓑ although ⓒ before ⓓ Since
17. Although happiness may seem far away
18. ④ 19. Though(Although)
20. not only, but also
21. She stopped eating junk food so that she could stay healthy.
22. ⑤
23. because/since/as she helped the poor
24. ③
25. (1) I don't know whether(if) I am tall enough to ride this roller coaster.
(2) I'm not sure whether(if) I passed the test or not. / I'm not sure whether or not I passed the test.

Chapter 07 관계사

핵심만 콕! 문법 Check

Point 1, 2

A 1. which 2. whom 3. whose 4. what 5. what 6. that

B 1. that 2. that 3. that 4. O

C 1. which was titled Using Energy
2. who(m) she met at the park
3. whose hair is grey

D 1. Everything that he had told us
2. He's the tallest boy that I have ever seen
3. what we should do
4. what I saw

Point 3-5

A 1. that 2. which 3. whom 4. X 5. who was

B 1. whom 2. which 3. which 4. X, which, that 5. who, that 6. in which 7. X, who, whom, that

C 1. which 2. Seoul, which is
3. his friend Jane, who was
4. which is in Paris

D 1. holding flowers is 2. written in English

Point 6-8

A 1. how 2. which 3. which 4. when 5. where 6. which

B 1. the reason 2. how 3. when 4. where

C 1. Whichever 2. who(m)ever 3. Whoever

D 1. whatever you know
2. whoever knocks
3. however rich they are

내신 만점! 실전 기출

01. ①	02. ②	03. ⑤	04. ③
05. ③	06. ②		

07. Imagine all the fossils that we will see
08. Whatever 09. ① 10. ②
11. where 12. ①
13. sent by my uncle was very interesting
14. ③ 15. the Greek myth, which
16. the way 17. ③ 18. ③ 19. ②
20. ③ 21. ③
22. Tell me the reason for which you came to class very late.
23. ② 24. ②
25. (1) who(that), made (2) what, invented

Chapter 08 가정법

핵심만 콕! 문법 Check

Point 1, 2

A 1. were 2. were not 3. would allow
4. could 5. would go

B 1. have liked 2. had seen
3. had known 4. wouldn't have been
5. hadn't had

C 1. Tony knew the problem
2. I were in your shoes
3. the weather wasn't, didn't swim
4. I didn't study, couldn't get

D 1. If he didn't have an appointment, he would
2. If I had had breakfast, I wouldn't have been
3. If I were born again, I would become
4. If he had practiced a lot, he would have won

Point 3-6

A 1. could 2. had not been
3. were able to 4. had solved

B 1. Without 2. will 3. knew
4. could 5. were 6. were

C 1. I had enough time
2. as if he were a main actor
3. Without(But for)
4. Had they practiced harder

D 1. could go there
2. as if she had gotten well
3. If I were you, would study
4. But for the laws, would be
5. If he had not been injured, would have been

내신 만점! 실전 기출

01. ⑤ **02.** ⑤
03. (1) were (2) had (3) make
04. I would yell/ run away/ climb up a tree/ hold my breath/ lie with my face down on the ground.
05. As, don't work, can't
06. I were not, could go **07.** ② **08.** ④
09. (1) But for, could not get
(2) were not for, could not get
10. ④ **11.** ③
12. as if he were a native speaker
13. ① **14.** ④ **15.** ③ **16.** ④
17. (A) as if, knew (B) as if, were not
18. I wish I got straight A's. **19.** ④ **20.** ④
21. If I had finished, could go **22.** ⑤
23. as if, were
24. If she had not worked so hard, she could not have become the Sales Queen.
25. (1) were sunny, we could go to the zoo
(2) I could have a birthday party

MEMO